Advances in Optimization and Linear Programming

Advances in Optimization and Linear Programming

Ivan Stanimirović

First edition published 2022

Apple Academic Press Inc.
1265 Goldenrod Circle, NE,
Palm Bay, FL 32905 USA

4164 Lakeshore Road, Burlington,
ON, L7L 1A4 Canada

CRC Press
6000 Broken Sound Parkway NW,
Suite 300, Boca Raton, FL 33487-2742 USA

2 Park Square, Milton Park,
Abingdon, Oxon, OX14 4RN UK

© 2022 Apple Academic Press, Inc.

Apple Academic Press exclusively co-publishes with CRC Press, an imprint of Taylor & Francis Group, LLC

Library and Archives Canada Cataloguing in Publication

Title: Advances in optimization and linear programming / Ivan Stanimirović.

Names: Stanimirović, Ivan, author.

Description: First edition. | Includes bibliographical references and index.

Identifiers: Canadiana (print) 20210285362 | Canadiana (ebook) 20210285389 | ISBN 9781774637401 (hardcover) | ISBN 9781774637418 (softcover) | ISBN 9781003256052 (ebook)

Subjects: LCSH: Linear programming—Mathematical models.

Classification: LCC T57.76 .S73 2022 | DDC 519.7/2—dc23

Library of Congress Cataloging-in-Publication Data

Names: Stanimirović, Ivan, author.

Title: Advances in optimization and linear programming / Ivan Stanimirović.

Description: First edition. | Palm Bay, FL : Apple Academic Press, 2022. | Includes bibliographical references and index. | Summary: "This new volume provides the information needed to understand the simplex method, the revised simplex method, dual simplex method, and more for solving linear programming problems. Following a logical order, the book first gives a mathematical model of the linear problem programming and describes the usual assumptions under which the problem is solved. It gives a brief description of classic algorithms for solving linear programming problems as well as some theoretical results. It goes on to explain the definitions and solutions of linear programming problems, outlining the simplest geometric methods, and showing how they can be implemented. Practical examples are included along the way. The book concludes with a discussion of multi-criteria decision-making methods. This volume is a highly useful guide to linear programming for professors and students in optimization and linear programming"-- Provided by publisher.

Identifiers: LCCN 2021037727 (print) | LCCN 2021037728 (ebook) | ISBN 9781774637401 (hardcover) | ISBN 9781003256052 (ebook)

Subjects: LCSH: Linear programming. | Simplexes (Mathematics) | Mathematical optimization.

Classification: LCC T57.76 .S83 2022 (print) | LCC T57.76 (ebook) | DDC 519.7/2--dc23

LC record available at https://lccn.loc.gov/2021037727

LC ebook record available at https://lccn.loc.gov/2021037728

ISBN: 978-1-77463-740-1 (hbk)
ISBN: 978-1-77463-741-8 (pbk)
ISBN: 978-1-00325-605-2 (ebk)

About the Author

Ivan Stanimirović, PhD, is currently working as an Associate Professor at the Department of Computer Science, Faculty of Sciences and Mathematics at the University of Niš, Serbia. He was formerly with the Faculty of Management at Megatrend University, Belgrade, as a Lecturer. His work spans from multi-objective optimization methods to applications of generalized matrix inverses in areas such as image processing and restoration and computer graphics. His current research interests include computing generalized matrix inverses and their applications, applied multi-objective optimization and decision making, as well as deep learning neural networks. Dr. Stanimirović was the Chairman of a workshop held at the 13th Serbian Mathematical Congress, Vrnjačka Banja, Serbia, in 2014.

Contents

Preface

In the first part of this book, we give a mathematical model of linear problem programming and describe the usual assumptions under which the problem is solved. Below is a brief description of classic algorithms for solving linear programming problems and some theoretical results. Proofs of the theorem can be found in standard monographs and linear textbooks programming and optimization from the literature list. Then, we will study the definition and solution of linear programming problems. That is what it entails first mathematical model and basic definitions and basic properties of a set of permissible solutions. We will then outline the simplest geometric method for solving the linear problem programming and show how it can be implemented.

In the second chapter, we will study the simplex method for solving the linear programming problem in general form, and we will detail its stages and the dual simplex method. We will also consider another version called the simplex method and the revised simplex method to resolve the problem of numerical stability of the classical simplex method. Finally, we will point to the problem of cycling and two ways to overcome this problem. We will also show that it is a simplex algorithm of exponential complexity, despite its excellent properties on practical problems.

The third chapter presents the results from the work [43, 54], and deals with modifications and refinements of particular stages of simplex methods. In Ref. [54], this algorithm was used, since it does not require the introduction of artificial variables. In this chapter, two algorithms were introduced to obtain an initial basic permissible solution in phase I of the two-phase simplex algorithm (described in Refs. [40] and [55]). A new rule is described for the choice of basic and non-basic variables to select the variable that enters the base and the variable that leaves the base. At the end of this chapter, we will detail the implementation of the simplex and revised simplex method.

In the final chapter, the post-optimal analysis of simplex methods is studied, and multi-criteria decision-making methods are listed, and final remarks are provided.

Chapter 1

Introduction

Mathematical programming problems occur in different disciplines. For example, a stock market manager has to choose the investments that will generate the highest possible profit at an opportunity; this puts the risk of large losses at a predetermined level. The production manager organizes production at the factory so that the quantity of products and the quality are maximum, and the consumption of materials and time are minimum, with limited resources (number of workers, machine capacity, and opening hours). A scientist makes a mathematical model of the physical process which best describes a particular physical occurrence, and has a finite number of measurement results available. Also, the model should not be too complicated.

Operations research is a branch of mathematics consistent in the use of mathematical, statistical, and algorithms in order to carry out a process of decision-making models. It often deals with the study of complex real systems, in order to improve (or optimize) the operation of the same. Operations research enables analysis of decision-making, given the scarcity of resources to determine how they can maximize or minimize them.

In mathematics and computer science, an algorithm is a step-by-step procedure used to perform calculations. Algorithms are used for computing, data processing, and automatic locking. More precisely, an algorithm is an efficient method expressed by a final list of defined instructions. Start the pipe from the initial step and the entrance (which can be empty). The instructions describe the calculation, which after execution leads to a finite number of successive steps, giving the output in the last step. The complexity of an algorithm can be described as the number of primitive operations or basic steps that need to be performed. For certain input data, see the analysis of algorithms in Ref. [11].

The symbolic expression is a concept that denotes the use of computer tools for the transformation of mathematical symbols. It can be used to compute explicit results without numerical errors. That is why symbolic expression always expressed applies to conditioned problems. These can be rational functions or polynomials of one or more variables. There are several different computer algebra software packages that support symbolic computing, such as MATHEMATICA, MAPLE, MATLAB.

Traditional programming languages are procedural languages. The procedural program is written as a list of instructions, which are executed step-by-step by reading Zotos. Programs in procedural computer languages such as C can be used in calculations, but are limited in cost in understanding more complex algorithms, because they give little information about the steps. Many researchers use the ability to develop "rapid-prototype" code to test the behavior of the algorithm before investing effort in developing code for the algorithm in a procedural language. The approach with MATHEMATICA has great advantages in researching over procedural programming available in MAPLE and in procedural languages. MATHEMATICA allows several program paradigms: object-oriented, procedural, symbolic, and functional programming. Our main goal of the research was to develop algorithms suitable for implementation both in MATHEMATICA and in procedural programming languages.

Although linear programming is very applicable in practice, many problems in practice cannot be adequately linearized without while the drastically does not lose on accuracy. In this case, nonlinear programming methods are applied. In addition to nonlinearity, in many problems, it is necessary to find the optimum of more than one objective function. In that case, we need to solve ***the problem of multiobjective optimization.*** If all , the goal functions have an optimum at the same point, the problem is trivial and comes down directly to the problem of nonlinear or linear programming. In practice, this situation is very rare. There are several methods for rescuing problems multiobjective optimization [36]. Common to all these methods is that the initial problem in the appropriate way is to reduce the problem of linear and nonlinear programming.

Higher sectoral criteria optimization can be seen as a continuation of research in the classroom (single-criteria) optimization along with some extensions. Formally, the basic extension is the introduction of a vector criterion function, which leads to the vector maximum problem. Essentially, it is necessary to expand the concept of optimality. Considering the problem of the vector maximum, the concept of optimality is replaced by the concept of noninferiority (Pareto optimality). The notion of a general (unique) optimization criterion can be introduced, which includes criterion functions and decision-makers. The solution of the multiobjective optimization problem obtained according to such a criterion is optimal. In this case, the notion of the optimal solution from the classical optimization can be retained in the higher sectoral one. However, these difficulties will only arise when trying to formalize such a unique criterion. Therefore, two phases or stages are used in multiobjective optimization. In the first phase, a set of "better" solutions is determined on the basis of a vector criterion function. And in the second phase, based on the preference of the decision-maker, the final decision is adopted, which can be called optimal. The set of decisions presented to the decision-maker should contain a small number of decisions, which are non-inferior to the given criterion functions. The problem of multi-sector optimization occurs most often in the planning of complex systems; for example, regional development, development of water or electricity systems, urban planning, and preservation of the natural environment [38]. The higher securitization problem occurs in economics as a problem of determining the market equilibrium [38]. A similar problem arises as a problem of equilibrium in game theory. In game theory, games are considered in which decision theory appears as "group decision making" or decision making with several decision-makers.

In this chapter, we will present the problem of multi-sector optimization, as well as the means for its solution. We will first give a definition of the problem of multiobjective optimization as well as necessary terms for later consideration. Theoretically, we will process and implement several classical methods of multi-criteria optimization. Each of the described methods will be illustrated by one or more examples. Implementation considerations methods are original and are taken from the works [57].

The general formulation of multiobjective optimization (MOO) has the general form:

$$\begin{array}{ll} \max & Q(\mathbf{x}) = Q_1(\mathbf{x}), \ldots, Q_l(\mathbf{x}), \quad \mathbf{x} \in \mathbb{R}^n \\ \text{p.o.} & f_i(\mathbf{x}) \leq 0, \; i = 1, \ldots, m \qquad\qquad (1.0.1) \\ & h_i(\mathbf{x}) = 0, \; i = 1, \ldots, k. \end{array}$$

where; $Q_1(\mathbf{x}), \ldots, Q_l(\mathbf{x})$, $f_1(x), \ldots, f_m(x), g_1(x), \ldots, g_m(x)$ are the real functions of n variables contained in the vector $\mathbf{x} = (x_1, \ldots, x_n)$.

This task looks for a solution to $\mathbf{x}$ that maximizes all 1 functions of the target. That is why the task of multiobjective optimization (MOO) is also called the vector optimization task. Because of simplicity only maximization problems are considered here. It is known that the task of minimization simply translates into the task of maximization by multiplication criterion functions with -1. All further presented definitions and methods are possible to adjust and solve the minimization task.

We say that $\mathbf{X} \subseteq R^n$ *is a set of admissible shadows* if:

$$\mathbf{X} = \{\mathbf{x} | f_i(\mathbf{x}) \leq 0, \; i = 1, \ldots, m; \; h_i(\mathbf{x}) = 0, \; i = 1, \ldots, k\}.$$

Each admissible solution $\mathbf{x} \in \mathbf{X}$ corresponds to a set of criteria values function, i.e., vector $Q(\mathbf{x}) = (Q_1(\mathbf{x}), Q_2(x), \ldots, Q_l(\mathbf{x}))$. In that way, the set of admissible solutions is mapped to the *criterion set*, i.e., $S = \{Q(\mathbf{x}) | \mathbf{x} \in \mathbf{X}\}$.

In the following text, the following terms will be used:

- *Marginal solutions* of the MOO task is determined by by optimizing each of the goal functions individually over the given one permissible set, i.e., solving l one objective tasks:

$$\text{max} \quad Q_j(\mathbf{x}), \quad \mathbf{x} \in \mathbb{R}^n$$
$$\text{p.o.} \quad f_i(\mathbf{x}) \leq 0, \quad i = 1, \ldots, m$$
$$h_i(\mathbf{x}) = 0, \quad i = 1, \ldots, k.$$

We will mark marginal solutions with $\mathbf{x}^{(j)^*} = (x_1^{(j)^*}, x_2^{(j)^*}, \ldots, x_n^{(j)^*})$, where; $x^{(j)^*}$ is the optimal solution obtained by optimizing the j-th objective function over a given allowable set $\mathbf{X}$.

- The ideal values of the objective functions, denoted by the prices with Q_j^* are the values of objective functions for marginal solutions

$$Q_j^* = Q_j(\mathbf{x}^{(j)^*}), \ae = 1, \ldots, l.$$

- The ideal values of the goal functions determine the *ideal point* in the criterion space, i.e., ideal value of the vector function

$$Q^* = (Q_1^*, Q_2^*, \ldots, Q_l^*).$$

- If there is a solution $\mathbf{x}^*$ that simultaneously maximizes all functions of the target, i.e.:

$$\mathbf{x}^* = \{\mathbf{x}|Q_j(\mathbf{x}) = Q_j^*, \ j = 1, \ldots, l\},$$

then such a word is called *perfect hay solution*.

In most cases, the marginal word shadow differs and the perfect word shadow does not exist. When a perfect solution exists, then it is not really a MOO problem.

It is very important to keep in mind that in real problems, the goals are over always in collision, which means that not everyone can be fully reached. It is not possible to strictly define the optimum nor for every two words formally determine which is better than the other. For this reason, the process of obtaining a solution requests the influence of the decision maker (hereinafter DM). This is the best thing for someone who has a deeper insight into the problem, and according to whose request, the solution is approached. Bearers decisions can be made, and then the problem can be further complicated because of their different goals, participation in decision-making and the degree of responsibility they are willing to take on.

The fact that the tasks of the MOO, as a rule, do not have a perfect meaning to reconsider the concept of optimality and the definition of the optimal solution. The concept of *Pareto optimality* plays a key role in this. It is an expansion of the known concept of optimality used in classical single-criterion optimization.

Pareto optimum is defined as follows:

Definition 1.0.1. *The admissible solution* $\mathbf{x}^*$ *represents Pareto optimum if there is no other admissible solution* $\mathbf{x}$ *such that:*

$$Q_j(\mathbf{x}) \geq Q_j(\mathbf{x}^*) \quad \forall j = 1, \ldots, l$$

where at least one of the inequalities turns into a strict inequality $>$.

In other words, $\mathbf{x}$ is Pareto optimum if it would improve the value of any target function caused a deterioration in the value of another target function. For Pareto optimum, there are the following synonyms: *efficient, dominant,* and *non-dominant solution.*

In addition to the Pareto optimum, weak and strict (strong) Pareto optimums are defined.

Definition 1.0.2. *The admissible solution* $\mathbf{x}^*$ *is weak Pareto optimum if there is no one another admissible solution* x *such that*

$$Q_j(\mathbf{x}) > Q_j(\mathbf{x}^*) \quad \forall j = 1, \ldots, l.$$

In other words, $\mathbf{x}^*$ is a weak Pareto optimum if it cannot at the same time improve all target functions.

Definition 1.0.3. *The Pareto optimal solution* $\mathbf{x}^*$ *is strict Pareto optimum if there is a the number* $\beta > 0$ *such that for each index* $j \in \{1, \ldots, l\}$ *and for each* $\mathbf{x}$ *which satisfies the condition:*

$$Q_j(\mathbf{x}) > Q_j(\mathbf{x}^*)$$

there is at least one $i \in \{1, \ldots, l\} \setminus \{j\}$ *such that:*

$$Q_i(\mathbf{x}) > Q_i(\mathbf{x}^*)$$

and that it is valid
$$\frac{Q_j(\mathbf{x}) - Q_j(\mathbf{x}^*)}{Q_i(\mathbf{x}^*) - Q_i(\mathbf{x})} \geq \beta.$$

The strict Pareto optimum is distinguished by the Pareto solution that does not change causes excessive relative changes in goal functions.

The relation between the described optimums is such that each set of stricter Pareto optimum is a subset of weaker optimums, i.e., every Pareto is the optimum at the same time a weak Pareto optimum, and every strict Pareto optimum is also a Pareto optimum.

1.1 Multiobjective Optimization

In multi-criteria optimization, several opposing goal functions should be reduced to a minimum at the same time respecting the given restrictions:

$$\text{Max.:} \quad Q(\mathbf{x}) = \{Q_1(\mathbf{x}), \ldots, Q_l(\mathbf{x})\}, \quad \mathbf{x} \in \mathbf{R}^n$$

$$\text{p.o.:} \quad f_i(\mathbf{x}) \leq 0, \ i = 1, \ldots, m \qquad (1.1.2)$$

$$h_i(\mathbf{x}) = 0, \ i = 1, \ldots, k.$$

It is possible to construct an interval (often called a constraint) in ($refMOO$); we simply denote by $\mathbf{X}$. Thus, the whole $\mathbf{X}$ is defined by $\mathbf{X} = \{\mathbf{x}|f_i(\mathbf{x}) \leq 0, \ i = 1, \ldots, m; \ h_i(\mathbf{x}) = 0, \ i = 1, \ldots, k\}$.

As a consequence, the notation $\mathbf{xX}$ will indicate that $\mathbf{x}$ satisfies the inequality and equality of boundaries in (1.0.1). With $\mathbf{x_j}^*$ we denote the point that maximizes the j-th function of the target depending on the constraint $\mathbf{x} \in \mathbf{X}$.

In general, there is no special point that maximizes all target functions at once. For these reasons, a possible point is constructed as optimal if there is no possible point with the same or goal function being estimated. So that the true increase has the minimum value of the target function. For the sake of completeness, we redefine the definitions of non-inferior solution (Pareto-optimal solution) and ideal (utopia) point from Refs. [12], [34], and [35].

Definition 1.1.1. *Solution* $\mathbf{x}^*$ *is said to be Pareto optimal solution multiobjective optimization problems* (1.0.1) *if there is no other pos-*

sible revision of $\mathbf{x} \in \mathbf{X}$ *so that* $Q_j(\mathbf{x}) \geq Q_j(\mathbf{x}^*)$ *for every* $j = 1, \ldots, l,$ *and* $Q_j(\mathbf{x}) > Q_j(\mathbf{x}^*)$ *for at least one index* j.

Definition 1.1.2. *A point* $\mathbf{x}^0$ *is the ideal point of the problem* (1.0.1) *of the problem if and only if:*

$$Q_i(\mathbf{x}^0) = \max_{\mathbf{x}}\{Q_i(\mathbf{x})| \ \mathbf{x} \in \mathbf{X}\}, \ i = 1, \ldots, l.$$

The multicriteria problem is often solved by combining multiple goals in one goal, which solution is Pareto optimal point for the original problem.

The following optimization tools are available:

1. Compiled programming languages (Fortran 90, C, etc.) with subroutine libraries (NAG, IMSL, etc.)

2. Interactive mathematical software: fast to define, solve, and prototype small problems, less efficient for large ones: a. General tools for numerical analysis (Matlab, IDL); b. Symbolic mathematical computer systems (Mathematica, Maple, Macsyma); c. Modeling tools for optimization (GAMS, AMPL).

One of the goals of our research was the implementation of the main methods of multi-sector optimization in computer algebraic system MATHEMATICA. The software package MATHEMATICA is one of the various programming languages available today, and is applicable to symbolic languages, and for numerical calculations Maeder, Wol. Several functions for limiting the cost of numerical optimization are available in the software package MATHEMATICA (see [33], [70]).

The *Maximize* and *Minimize* functions allow a specification of the maximization and minimization goal function, along with a set of constraints. In all cases, it is assumed that all variables are price limits that do not have negative values.

`Minimize[f, {cons}, {x, y,...}]` or `Minimize[{f, cons}, {x,` `y,...}]`, minimize f in the area specified by *cons*;

`Maximize [f, {cons }, {x, y, ... }]` or `Maximize[{f,cons },` `{x, y, ...}]`, find a maximum of f, in the area specified by *cons*.

`Minimize` and `Maximize` can be used to properly solve any polynomial programming problem function in which the functions of the goal f and the constraints *cons* include arbitrary polynomial functions of the variables [70]. An important feature of `Minimize` and `Maximize` is that they always find global minima and maxima [70].

The *NMinimize* and *NMaximize* functions implement several algorithms for finding global optimum constraints. Expressions:

`NMaximize[{f,cons}, vars, Method -> {method, mopts}]`,

`NMinimize[{f,cons}, vars, Method -> {method, mopts}]`,

find the global maximum and minimum, respectively, for the objective functions f by the constraint prices *cons*, using the method with optimization methods *method* with the method options defined in *mopts*.

1.2 Symbolic Transformations in Multi-Sector Optimization

The main details of multi-sector optimization that are specific to symbols and the expressions are described in the paper [57]. The implementation was performed in the software package `MATHEMATICA`. The method of weight coefficients, the main priority methods, and the method of target programming are discussed. The symbolic conversion of given goal functions and constraints into the corresponding problem of one goal function is treated in particular. Transformations from multiobjective to one-criteria problem u procedural programming languages are actually combinations of real values, and involve procedures that depend on the function of the goal. In our implementation, these transformations are performed in symbolic form by taking combinations of target functions, which include undefined symbols and unmarked variable prices.

We will suggest the following clear benefits that will result from the implementation problems of multiobjective optimization in the symbolic programming language MATHEMATICA, respect the traditional implementation in procedural programming languages.

1. Possibility to use arbitrary target functions and limitations (which are not defined by subroutines) during the execution of the implementation function. The main aspects of these advantages are:

   (i) The problem of secretory optimization (1.0.1) is represented by a suitable *in its form*, whose elements can be used prices as formal parameters in the optimization software. Inside the dream form of the problem (1.0.1) is an edited triple

   $$\{Q_1(\mathbf{x}), \ldots, Q_l(\mathbf{x})\},$$
   $$\{f_1(\mathbf{x}) \leq 0, \ldots, f_m(\mathbf{x}) \leq 0, h_1(\mathbf{x}) = 0, \ldots, h_k(\mathbf{x}) = 0\},$$
   $$\{x_1, \ldots, x_n\} \qquad\qquad (1.2.\ 1)$$

   The first element of the inner form, denoted by q, is a list $\{Q_1(\mathbf{x}), \ldots, Q_l(\mathbf{x})\}$ whose elements indefinite expressions representing goal functions. The second element in (1.2.1) is the constraint list $f_i(\mathbf{x}) \leq 0$, $i = 1, \ldots, m$, $h_i(\mathbf{x}) = 0$, $i = 1, \ldots, k$. We will label this argument as *constr*. The third element, labeled *var*, is a generic list of variables $\{x_1, \ldots, x_n\}$, determined on the basis of $\mathbf{x}$. In this sense, it is allowed that some arguments in $\mathbf{x}$ can be defined in global environment MATHEMATICA kernela.

(ii) If f is the objective function of the one-criteria optimization problem obtained from (1.2. 1), we can calculate its maximum using the standard function *Maximize*:

Maximize [f, constr, var].

The possibility of software to process arbitrary target functions at arbitrary constraints enables the application of all optimization models.

2. Possibility to use arrays of functions, whose elements can be select and later apply to the given arguments. These structures are not inherent in procedural programming languages.

Each expression contains in the list $q = \{Q_1(\mathbf{x}), \ldots, Q_l(\mathbf{x})\}$ can be immediately applied to the given arguments. It is possible to calculate the value of the function $q[[[]]]$ in point $x0$ using the transformation rules q[[i]] /. X -> X0 or q[[i]] /. Thread [Rule [x, x0]]. MATHEMATICA searches for parts of the function q[[i]] that can be replaced using the specified rule, and then performs a replacement.

Also, it is possible to define a function that takes another function as an argument, for example: pf[f_, x_]: = f[x] + f[1-x]. Later, expressions such as pf[q[[i]], x0] can be used. In the expression $f[x]$, the name of the function f is also expression, and can be treated as any numeric expression [70]. In particular, any element from q can be taken as an argument in the functions `Minimize` and `Maximize`.

3. An effective and natural symbolic transformation from a multi-criteria model to a corresponding one-criterion model.

Many optimization methods are based on sub-algorithms that require the construction of goal functions of general form.

$$G\left(q(\mathbf{x}), \Phi(f(\mathbf{x}), h(\mathbf{x}), \lambda)\right),$$

where; λ is a possible set of larger variables, and Φ is an arbitrary function.

Transformation of multiobjective to the one-criterion problem in procedural languages is basically a combination of real values. We will perform these transformations in symbolic form, using combinations of unexpressed expressions and symbols.

1.3　Pareto Optimality Test

As a rule, it is impossible to find a complete infinite set of Pareto optimal solutions to special problems from real life. For this reason, the engineering securitization problem of the command seeks to determine a subset of criterion-wise different Pareto optimal solutions finally. Also, there are a number of methods for proving Pareto optimality. These methods can also be used to find the original Pareto optimal solution of [?].

An algorithm for determining the Pareto optimality was introduced in the paper [57] solutions of multiobjective of the problem, using direct proof in accordance with the Pareto definition of the optimal point.

Algoritam 1.1 Pareto optimality test of fixed point $\mathbf{x}^*$.

Require: Optimization problem (1.0.1). Arbitrary fixed point $\mathbf{x}^*$.

1: Specify the set $X =$ `Reduce [constr /. List -> And, var]` and set *Optimal = true*.

2: For each index $j = 1, \ldots, l$ repeat Steps 2.1 and 2.2:

    2.1: Generate the following conjunction constraint

$$Par = X \text{ \&\& } u_1(\mathbf{x}) \text{ \&\& } \ldots \text{ \&\& } u_l(\mathbf{x}) \qquad (1.3.1)$$

  where

$$u_i(\mathbf{x}) = \begin{cases} Q_i(\mathbf{x}) \geq Q_i(\mathbf{x}^*), \ j \neq i, \\ Q_i(\mathbf{x}) > Q_i(\mathbf{x}^*), \ j = i. \end{cases} \qquad (1.3.2)$$

    2.2: If $Par = \emptyset$, set *Optimal := false* and to Step 3.

3: **return** the value of the variable *Optimal* as a result.

The corresponding function in our implementation is:

`IsPareto[q _List, constr _List, var _List, sol _List],`

where the formal parameters are taken in the following sense:

`q, constr, var`: internal representation of the problem of sector criteria optimization (1.0.1);

`sol`: The solution to the corresponding one-goal optimization problem.

Calling this function is a form:

`IsPareto[q, constr, var, First[Rest[Maximize[fun, constr, var]]]];`

where; fun, constr, and var are the representation of the corresponding one-target optimization problem.

In this function we use the following version of the standard MATHEMATICA functions Reduce and FindInstance [70]:

Reduce [expr, var] finds all real values of variables contained in the list var which satisfies a set of numbers containing logical connections and invariant polynomial equations and inequalities.

FindInstance [expr, var] determines the values of the variables from var in which the assertion is expr *true*. If no value is found for var, the result is an empty list. The expr parameter can contain equations, inequalities, a specification area, and quantifiers (see Ref. [70]).

```
Algebra 'InequalitySolve'
IsPareto[q_List, constr_List, var_List, res_List] : =
  Module[{X = {}, l = Length[q]},
    X = Reduce[constr/.{List->And}, var]; Ok = 1;
                                            (* Korak 1. *)
    For[j = 1, j < = l, j++,                 (* Korak 2. *)
      Par = X;
      For[i = 1, i < = l, i++,    (* Korak 2.1. *)
          If [j ! = i, Par = Par && q[[i]] > = (q[[i]]/. res),
                    Par = Par && q[[i]] > (q[[i]]/. res)
          ];
      ]; (* Par is of the form (4.1), (4.2) *)
      If[FindInstance[Par, var] ! = {}, Ok = 0; Break[]];
                                            (* Korak 2.2. *)
      (*If a var instance is found, abort the loop*)
    ];
    If[Ok = = 1,
        Print["Solution", {q/.res, res}, "is Pareto optimal"],
```

```
      Print["Solution", {q/.res, res}, "is not Pareto optimal"];
   ];
     Return[Ok]; (* Step 3. *)
 ]
```

1.4   The Method of Weight Coefficients

Weight coefficient method is the oldest method used for MOO. According to this method, the weight coefficient w_i is introduced for all criterion functions $Q_i(\ mathbf{x})$, $i = 1$, $ldots, l$, so the problem optimization reduces to the following scalar optimization:

$$\max \quad Q(\mathbf{x}) = \sum_{i=1}^{l} w_i Q_i(\mathbf{x}) \qquad (1.4.1)$$

$$\text{p.o.} \quad \mathbf{x} \in \mathbf{X},$$

where; w_i, $i = 1$, $ldots, l$ meet the following conditions:

$$\sum_{i=1}^{l} w_i = 1, \quad w_i \geq 0, \ i = 1, \ldots, l.$$

The method of weight coefficients is often used by setting the values of these coefficients. However, this always causes certain difficulties and objections to this procedure, because the subjective influence on the final solution is entered through the given values of the weight coefficients.

The main idea in the method of weight coefficients is to choose weight coefficients w_i that correspond to target functions $Q_i(\mathbf{x})$,

$i = 1, \ldots, l$. Many authors have developed systematic approaches in weight selection, the review of which can be found in Refs. [23], [24], and [63]. One of the advantages of this method is that the variation of weights is consistent and continuous; it does not always have to result in an accurate and complete representation of the Pareto optimal set. This shortcoming has been discussed in Ref. [17].

Theorem 1.4.1. *If all weight coefficients w_i are positive, then the solution of the problem* (1.4.1) *is Pareto optimal solution of the initial MOO problem.*

Proof. Let $\mathbf{x}^*$ solve the problem (1.4.1), and let all weight coefficients be strictly positive. Suppose that it is not Pareto optimal, i.e., there exists $\mathbf{x} \in S$ so for $i = 1, \ldots, l$ it is valid $Q_i(\mathbf{x}) \geq Q_i(\mathbf{x}^*)$, where at least one strict inequality holds (say for the index j). As $w_i > 0$ for every i, it is valid

$$\sum_{i=1}^{l} w_i Q_i(\mathbf{x}) > \sum_{i=1}^{l} w_i Q_i(\ mathbf f x^*)$$

So we get a contradiction with the assumption that $\mathbf{x}^*$ is a shadow and problem (1.4.1). It follows that $\mathbf{x}^*$ Pareto is optimal. □

Theorem 1.4.2. *If for every $i \in \{1, \ldots, l\}$ the condition $w_i \geq 0$ is fulfilled, then the solution is problem* (1.4.1) *weak Pareto optimum of the initial MOO problem.*

Proof. Let $\mathbf{x}^*$ solve the problem (1.4.1) and that the condition $w_i \geq 0$ is satisfied. Suppose that it is not weak Pareto optimal, i.e., yes there is $\mathbf{x} \in S$ so that for $i = 1, \ldots, l$ it is valid $Q_i(\mathbf{x}) > Q_i(\mathbf{x}^*)$. All coefficients w_i are non-negative and at least one is strictly greater than zeros (due to $\sum_{i=1}^{l} w_i = 1$), so it is valid

$$\sum_{i=1}^{l} w_i Q_i(\mathbf{x}) > \sum_{i=1}^{l} w_i Q_i(\mathbf{x}^*)$$

So we get a contradiction with the assumption that $\mathbf{x}^*$ is a shadow of the weight problem. Thus, $\mathbf{x}^*$ is a weak Pareto optimum. $\square$

Theorem 1.4.3. *If the solution of the problem* (1.4.1) *is unique, then Pareto is also optimal.*

Proof. Let $\mathbf{x}^*$ be a unique solution to the problem (1.4.1). Suppose that it is not a Pareto optimal solution to the MOO problem, i.e., that there exists $\mathbf{x} \in S$ so that for $i = 1, \ldots, l$ it is valid $Q_i(x) \geq Q_i(x^*)$, where at least one strict inequality (say for index j). Note that it knows $\mathbf{x} \neq \mathbf{x}^*$. Since $w_i \geq 0$ for every i, it is valid

$$\sum_{i=1}^{l} w_i Q_i(\mathbf{x}) \geq \sum_{i=1}^{l} w_i Q_i(\mathbf{x}^*)$$

If a strict inequality were valid, then $\mathbf{x}^*$ would not be a solution to the problem (1.4.1). So your equality. This means that there are two different readings of $\mathbf{x}$ and $\mathbf{x}^*$ problem (1.4.1), which is a contradiction. $\square$

We will now show a strong assertion.

Theorem 1.4.4. *If all $w_i > 0$, $i \in \{1, \ldots, l\}$, then the solution of the problem* (1.4.1) *is a strict Pareto optimum of the MOO problem.*

Proof. Let $\mathbf{x}^*$ be the shadow of the weight problem. We have shown that Pareto is optimal. Prove in winter that this solution is also a strict Pareto optimum with a constant

$$M = (k-1) \max_{i,j} \frac{w_j}{w_i}.$$

Suppose the opposite, that exists $\mathbf{x} \in S$ and index i such that $Q_i(\mathbf{x}) > Q_i(\mathbf{x}^*)$ where for each j for which $Q_j(\mathbf{x}^*) > Q_j(\mathbf{x})$ it is true $Q_i(\mathbf{x}^*) - Q_i(\mathbf{x}) < M(Q_j(\mathbf{x}) - Q_j(\mathbf{x}^*))$. With change:

$$M = \frac{(k-1)w_j}{w_i}$$

We get:

$$w_i \frac{Q_i(\mathbf{x}^*) - Q_i(\mathbf{x})}{k-1} < w_j \left(Q_j(\mathbf{x}) - Q_j(\mathbf{x}^*)\right) > 0 \,.$$

So, for each $j \neq i$ for which it is true that $Q_j(\mathbf{x}^*) > Q_j(\mathbf{x})$. For index $j \neq i$ for which $Q_j(\mathbf{x}^*) \leq Q_j(\mathbf{x})$ the above inequality certainly holds. So, for each $j \neq i$ it is true.

$$w_i \frac{Q_i(\mathbf{x}^*) - Q_i(\mathbf{x})}{k-1} < w_j \left(Q_j(\mathbf{x}) - Q_j(\mathbf{x}^*)\right),$$

so by summing these inequalities for $j = 1, \ldots, i-1, i+1, \ldots, l$ we get:

$$w_i \left(Q_i(\mathbf{x}^*) - Q_i(\mathbf{x})\right) < \sum_{j=1, j \neq i}^{l} w_j \left(Q_j(\mathbf{x}) - Q_j(\mathbf{x}^*)\right)$$

that is:

$$\sum_{j=1}^{l} w_j Q_j(\mathbf{x}^*) < \sum_{j=1}^{l} w_j Q_j(\mathbf{x}) \,.$$

We get that $\mathbf{x}^*$ is not a solution to the weight problem, i.e., we are coming to the contradiction. We conclude that $\mathbf{x}^*$ is indeed a strict Pareto optimum of the initial problem. $\square$

The weight coefficient should in some way represent the value of the cross-function to which it is assigned. In order to achieve that, we must first normalize the criterion functions, that is to them change so that they have approximately equal values, while retaining all the essential properties. For example, if it is a criterion function linear $Q_j(\mathbf{x}) = \sum_{i=1}^{n} a_i x_i$, then normalized form of this function be:

$$\frac{Q_j(\mathbf{x})}{\sum_{i=1} n a_i}.$$

If the decision-maker himself defines the weight coefficients, then this method belongs to the group of a priori methods. However, little is usually known about how the odds should be chosen. Therefore, the usual weight problem is solved for various vector values $(w_1, \ldots, w_l)$ and in this way, they get different readings between the sentences in which DO chooses the one that suits him best. If this approach is used, then this method becomes a posteriori method.

The main disadvantage of this method is the difficulty of determining the weight coefficients when we do not have enough information about the problem. For this reason, we propose an algorithm for the automatic generation of weight coefficients in order to obtain Pareto optimal points. For positive weights and a convex problem, the optimal solutions of a single-criterion problem are Pareto optimal, i.e., minimizing the corresponding single-criteria problem is sufficient for Pareto optimality.

There are numerous operations research problems investigated and implemented at the moment. In [57], the implementation of polynomial multi-objective optimization has been analyzed in MATHE-MATICA. We developed a linear weighted sum method for multi-objective optimization problem and presented it in [60]. Also, we provided the so-called compendious lexicographic method for multi-objective optimization tasks in [59].

Many applications of operations research exist in everyday life and science and technology. For instance, an optimization algorithm for LED-based Vis-NIR spectrally tunable light source is examined in [32]. An application of the ELECTRE method to planetary gear train optimization is detailed in [50], and in [51] a model of planetary gear multicriteria optimization is further developed. We have also investigated the computation of some efficient locations of the Weber problem with barriers in [58]. Also, a heuristic algorithm for a single resource-constrained project scheduling problem based on the dynamic programming is investigated in [61].

Linear programming task is to determine the maximum (minimum) linear function that depends on multiple variables provided that these variables are nonnegative and satisfy linear restrictions in the form of equations and/or inequalities. The linear objective function to be optimized is called the *goal function* or target function. Linear programming is one of the most effective approaches to formulating and solving complex decision-making problems and, as such, is a fundamental discipline of operational research.

Linear programming does report in the field of solving practical tasks such as are economic development planning both at the work organization level so on the broader regional or broadest social plane.

It is generally accepted that it is the first work to belong linear programming published by L.V. Kantorovic in 1939 [26]. It defines the transport task for the first time. The first work in this area included the work of Colonel Vlastimir Ivanovic from 1940, entitled "Rules for the calculation of the required number of means of transport" [25]. In this paper, Colonel Ivanovic demonstrated how to calculate the minimum number of vehicles for transporting a given quantity of material using the "Principle of Economy." Linear models are also used in solving certain transport problems, which are known in theory and practice as transportation problems, and in other planning areas.

The first algorithm for solving the transport problem was elaborated by F. F. Hitchock in [22] in 1941. On the formulation of the transport problem and it's also worked with Koopmans, which is the results of his research published in 1947. The greatest contribution to the development of linear of programming was given by G.B. Dantzig, who formulated the general in 1947 linear programming problem and set up a simplex method. In [16], the basics of simplex methods are presented. The papers of John von Neumann from this period made it possible in theory formulating a dual problem as well as finding a connection between linear programming and game theory. Removal method degeneration is suggested in [9]. Also significant are the papers of Gass and Saaty in 1955. Fr. parametric programming as well as works by E. Beale and R. Gomory from 1958 on integer programming.

– Linear Programming

The linear programming is a mathematical method or algorithm by which an undetermined problem is solved, formulated by linear equations, optimizing the objective function, also linear.

The linear programming is to optimize (minimize or maximize) a linear function, which we call objective function, such that the variables of the function are subject to a number of constraints expressed by a system of linear inequalities.

The variables are real numbers greater than or equal to zero. If it is required that the resulting value of the variable is an integer, the resolution procedure is called integer programming. This is the kind of programming that will be used to solve the problem that concerns us, because the solution will be "number of sheets" to cut a certain way, and veneers are a whole variable type.

– Excel Solver

It serves for solving linear and nonlinear optimization. You can also specify restrictions on integer decision variables. Solver can solve problems with up to 200 decision variables, 100 explicit constraints, and 400 simple (upper and lower bounds or integer restrictions on variables decision). The literature is a link to an online manual in a pdf file that explains how to use the excel solver function.

From the year 1949, a number of publications listed on the basis of the theory of linear programming and its applications to various branches of the economy. Deserve special mention for the decisive influence they had in the perfection and dissemination of these mathematical techniques, the work and activities of the Cowles Commission for Research in economics, the Rand Corporation, the Department of Mathematics at Princeton University, and the Carnegie Institute of Technology.

Moya (1998, p. 63) mentions that George B. Dantzig and another group of associated researchers in 1947, accepted the request of military authorities of the government of the United States, they set out to investigate how it could apply mathematics and statistics to solve problems of planning and progression for purely military purposes. In the same year, Dantzig and his colleagues raised for the first time the basic mathematical structure of the linear programming problem.

Generally speaking, one can say that any phenomenon involving a given nonnegative number of variables (i.e., variables whose value is positive or zero) can be linked together by relations of inequality or equality and reflect the limited or restrictions that the phenomenon presents in order to optimize an objective can be formulated as a mathematical programming model. If both the constraints and the objective function can be stated by linear expressions, we are facing a particular field of mathematical programming that denominates "linear programming."

In this case, the word "programming" does not refer to computer programming; but it is used as a synonym for planning. Linear programming deals with planning activities to obtain an optimal result, that is, the result that best achieves the specified target (as the mathematical model) between alternative solutions.

Weber (1984, p. 718), the linear programming problem is about maximizing or minimizing a linear function of several primary variables, called a goal function subject to a set of equalities or linear inequalities called constraints, with the further proviso that none of the variables can be negative. The latter can be seen when the problem requires, through the ingenious device of expressing the variable of interest as the difference of two non-negative variables.

Briefly, it stated that linear programming is a mathematical method of solving problems where the objective is to optimize (maximize or minimize) a result from selecting the values of a set of decision variables, respecting restrictions pertaining to availability resources, technical specifications, or other conditions that limit the freedom of choice.

As if we have a particular interest in linear programming, we can represent a production system using a model or matrix which include:

- Costs and revenues generated per unit of activity (objective function).

- Contributions and input and output requirements for each activity (coefficients input/output).

- Resource availability, technical specifications, and business to respect (the right-side values of the constraints).

Specifically, linear programming is a mathematical method to analyze and choose the best among many alternatives. In general terms, one can think of programming as a means to determine the best way to distribute a limited amount of resources in an attempt to achieve an expressible target to maximize or minimize a certain amount.

The general model of a programming problem consists of two linear important very parts: the objective function and constraints.

– **The Linear Objective Function**

The mathematical expression of the target is called the objective function, and the goal must be to maximize or minimize that expression.

The aim can be the maximization of some input variables, which may vary from gross or net income, depending on the model is structured. Linear programming can also be applied to problems of cost minimization, and these programs are based on a different set of criteria for optimization.

C1, C2, ..., coefficients Cn are the cost coefficients (known) or income, depending on the type of problem you're seeing resole. Moreover, y1, y2..., yn are the decision variables (variables, or activity levels) to be determined such that the target is reached within the constraints faced by the problem.

Restrictions, expressed by linear inequalities, are composed of technical coefficients (Aij), activities, or processes (yn), which are also taken into account in the target function and also the cellular levels or limitations (Bi). According to Beneke and Winterboer (1984, p. 25), there are three basic types of restrictions: "higher than" ($>=$) of "less than" ($<=$) or equal ($=$), and these can be classified due to their nature:

- Resource Constraints or Entries: As such may include land, capital, labor, and facilities.

- External Constraints: This kind includes concepts such as government area of land allocations, credit limits assigned to products or legal obligations.

- Subjective Restrictions: These are the restrictions imposed by the operator. Limits may be difficult to define, but often are real and significant in the planning process. Often restrictions come from their own personal goals or business of the glider. Among the limitations of this kind may include the following:

  - Limitations on the level of credit that the glider is ready to be utilized. It is often less than the amount lenders are displaced to contribute. The typical motivation for such kind of limitations is little explicit desire to avoid the hazards of debt.

- Restrictions risk level activities involving aspects related to highly variable income such as raising sheep or cattle.

- Minimum restrictions concerning the operator consider desirable for not properly direct income such as maintaining pure, dairy cows or crops to maintain the qualities of the breed cows field.

As for the application that has linear programming, Moya (1998, 63) indicates that some of the major problems that came to settle with this tool are located in three areas: (1) production management, (2) evaluation project, and (3) inversion and agricultural applications. We indicate that this list does not exhaust in any way the options that linear programming has proven to be an excellent tool to support decision-making.

In all these situations, we can identify three common terms [5]:

1. There is a global size (goal) that wants to be optimized (profit, the difference between model predictions and experimental data).

2. In addition to the global goal, there are usually additional requirements or constraints that must be met (limited risk, resources, model complexity).

3. There are certain sizes so that if their values are selected "good," they are also satisfied objective and limitations. These quantities are called optimization variables or parameters.

So, in order to set the problem of mathematical programming, we must:

1. Select one or more optimization variables;

2. Select the objective function f;

3. Form a constraint set.

After that, the class of problem to which the mathematicians obtained is identified the model belongs to, and the method for solving it is selected.

There are several methods for solving linear programming problems [5, 8]. The geometric method is applicable to problems with a number of variables $n = 2$ or when $n - m = 2$, where m is the number of constraints. In principle, the linear programming problem can be solved geometrically in the case of $n = 3$. The disadvantage of the geometric method is that it does not solve the general task of linear programming, but only some special cases. Until the first general method for solving linear programming, problems came American mathematician Danzing in 1947 [16]. This method is known as the simplex linear programming method. He also formulated a general form of a linear programming problem and gave an algorithm for solving it, known as the *simplex method*. Dantzig's work has circulated among experts for many years and served as a basis for all subsequent considerations of the problem linear programming. Although other methods have been found in the meantime, this method is still in use today through numerous modifications (see papers [6]). Both geometric and simplex methods seek maximum (minimum) target functions at the boundaries of the boundary region.

In the later period, alternative approaches to resolution emerge as linear programming problems. We mention the works which are used generalized inverses [45] as well as works by Conn [10] and Dax [18] that do not use the simplex method. However, the practice has shown that the simplex method is very effective, in 1972. V. Klee

(Kli) and G.L. Minty proved that it was not polynomial [28]. They constructed a simple example of a linear task programming where the admissible set is deformed n -dimensional cube with 2^n top, for which the simplex method with a standard choice of a leading element requires $2^n - 1$ iterative steps. The first polynomial algorithm for solving a problem of linear programming was given by Hacien in [27] in 1979. This has taken a major turn in the development of linear programming. Khatsian has shown that his ellipsoid method solves the problem linear programming for $O(n^4\Lambda)$ elementary arithmetic operation, where Λ is the number of bits required to write all the parameters problems (constraint matrices, target functions, and right-hand side constraints. Hezian solved a very important theoretical question. However, it turned out that the ellipsoid method was not applicable in practice. Testing has shown that the simplex method is far more efficient because it "rarely" reaches an upper limit of complexity, unlike ellipsoid methods, which often does. This conclusion led them to find new methods for solving linear programming problems that, in addition, to polynomial complexity, they also have practical applicability.

The first such method was proposed in 1984 by N. Karmarkar in his work on Karmakar. Karmarkar's algorithm solved some test cases and up to 50 times faster than simplex methods. Karmarkar's result sparked a real revolution in the development of this area. After the Karmarkar method, a whole family of methods emerged known as *internal methods*. Today, **primal-dual** intrinsic methods are dominant for solving linear programming problems [71]. Although polynomial methods were discovered, simplex the method is still used today, and is still alive through numerous modifications. The simplex method is much better than the inner point method on the so-called poorly conditioned problems, because of its slow but reliable convergence. Likewise, in practice, there is often a need for solving a class of related problems where the optimal solution is one of them that can be effectively used as a starting point to solve other problems. In this case, too, the simplex method is a better choice than the inner point method.

In addition to the theoretical results, software packages for solving linear programmed problems appeared, and which are based on theoretical results. These software packages have found wide application in practice.

Internal methods are divided into *primal, dual* and *primal-dual*. The primal methods solve the linear programming problem in standard form:

$$\min \quad d^T y,$$
$$\text{subj.} \quad Ay = \beta, \quad y \geq 0,$$

where A is a matrix of type $m \times n$, while a, β, and γ are vectors of the corresponding dimension. Dual problems solve a dual form problem:

$$\max \quad \beta^T y,$$
$$\text{subj.} \quad A^T y + p = \gamma, \quad p \geq 0.$$

Primal-dual methods work simultaneously with both primal and dual problems (primal-dual method). Today, primal-dual methods are dominant. These methods are described in [71]. Learn your method internally points for solving linear programming problems belong modern and modern trend in the world, which is already confirmed published monographs on polynomial methods, such as [5, 71]. In the last 10 years, a large number of papers have been published areas so that the bibliography has thousands of titles.

There are three tools for solving linear programming problems.

- Models: The formulation of problems in detailed mathematical terms.

- Algorithms: Techniques for solving models.

- Computers and Software: Machines for performing algorithmic steps.

There are a number of software packages that are designed to solve the problem of linear programming.

HOPDM is written in the programming language FORTRAN [21].

LIPSOL is written in MATLAB and FORTRAN. Part of the code relating to **Sparse Cholesky** factorization and solution of linear systems is written in FORTRAN and the rest of the code in MATLAB. The algorithm is described in [72].

LOQO is written in the programming language C and is described in [62].

PCx is written in C and programming languages FORTRAN. **Sparse Cholesky** code is written in FORTRAN and the rest of the code in C. A detailed description can be provided find [15].

MOSEK is written in the programming language C ++ and represents one of the strongest solvers not only for linear problems programming already in general for square and nonlinear programming. Unlike the previously mentioned program, this program is commercial.

LINDO-linear interactive and discrete optimizer-is an interactive software package that can be used to solve linear programming problems. It was developed in 1980 and has been around ever since, adapted to the Windows environment and graphically oriented applications. The LINDO software package is used to solve problems posed directly from the keyboard.

1.5 Mathematical Model

The implementation of some linear programming methods in the MATHEMATICA programming language can be found in [5]. The *General form* of linear programming problems can be expressed as follows. Determine the values of the variables $y_1, \ldots, y_k$ that match linear equations the inequalities

$$N_i^{(1)} : \quad \sum_{j=1}^{k} a_{ij} y_j \; \leq \; \beta_i, \quad i \in I_1$$

$$J_i : \quad \sum_{j=1}^{k} a_{ij} y_j \; = \; \beta_i, \quad i \in I_2 \qquad (1.5.0.1)$$

$$N_i^{(2)} : \quad \sum_{j=1}^{k} a_{ij} y_j \; \geq \; \beta_i, \quad i \in I_3$$

$$y_j \; \geq \; 0, \quad j \in J \subseteq \{1, \ldots, k\},$$

where $I_1 \cup I_2 \cup I_3 = \{1, \ldots, m\}$, $I_1 \cap I_2 = \emptyset$, $I_1 \cap I_3 = \emptyset$, $I_2 \cap I_3 = \emptyset$, so that the linear objective function

$$\omega(y) = \omega(y_1, \ldots, y_k) = \gamma_1 y_1 + \cdots + \gamma_k x_k \qquad (1.5.0.\ 2)$$

has an extremum, i.e., minimum or maximum. They are $\alpha_{ij}, \beta_i, \gamma_j$ known real numbers.

By convention, in the general case, a vector $y \in \mathbb{R}^k$ represents the $k-$ tuple of real numbers $y = (y_1, \ldots, y_k)$,, while matrix formulas imply that y is a matrix of type $k \times 1$ (vector), i.e.:

$$y = \begin{bmatrix} y_1 \\ \vdots \\ y_k \end{bmatrix}, \quad y^\tau = [y_1 \ldots y_k].$$

Next, $y \geq 0$ means $y_1 \geq 0, \ldots, y_k \geq 0$.

$y = (y_1, y_2, \ldots, y_k)$ solution in applications meaning of a plan or program (production, transportation), so this is the task named "programming" and the name "linear programming" indicates that the constraints of the variables (1.5.0. 1) as well as the objective function (1.5.0. 2) are linear.

An arbitrary solution of a system of inequalities (1.5.0. 1) can be think of the vector $y = (y_1, y_2, \ldots, y_k)$, which in geometric the interpretation represents the point of the k -dimensional space $\mathbb{R}^k$. We call each nonnegative solution to the system of inequalities (1.5.0. 1).

If we denote by Γ_P the set of admissible solutions, then Γ_P is a subset of R^k. For Γ_P, we assume that it is not empty and contains at least one element (case when task (1.5.0. 1)–(1.5.0. 2) has a solution).

Optimal solution $y^* = (y_1^*, \ldots, y_k^*)\Gamma_P$ task linear programming is the permissible solution for which function goal $\omega(y) = \omega(y_1, \ldots, y_k)$ reaches maximum (minimum). In the case of goal function maximization is a requirement

$$\omega(y^*) = \max_{y \in \Gamma_P} \omega(y)$$

or

$$\omega(y^*) \geq \omega(y) \quad \forall y \in \Gamma_P.$$

It is often sought in practice that the optimal value of the goal function is the smallest on the set of admissible solutions Γ_P. In this case, optimally $y^* \in \Gamma_P$ is the admissible solution for which it is fulfilled

$$\omega(y^*) = \min_{y \in \Gamma_P} \omega(y).$$

or

$$\omega(y^*) \leq \omega(y) \quad \forall y \in \Gamma_P.$$

In one specific task, only the maximization problem, that is, the minimization problem, is solved. The problem of the minimum can be transformed into the problem of the maximum (and vice versa) by simply multiplying the objective function by -1, using the following Proposition 1.5.1 result.

Proposition 1.5.1. *The optimization criterion can be given replace with the opposite, without this replacement affecting the optimal solution, that is, if for $y^* \in \Gamma_P$ satisfied*

$$\omega(y^*) = \max_{y \in \Gamma_P} \omega(y)$$

then

$$-\omega(y^*) = \min_{y \in \Gamma_P} [-\omega(y)]$$

and reverse.

Proof. By the assumption of the theorem, it is fulfilled

$$\omega(y^*) \geq \omega(y) \qquad \forall y \in \Gamma_P.$$

If we multiply this inequality sa -1, is obtained by:

$$-\omega(y^*) \leq -\omega(y) \qquad \forall y \in \Gamma_P,$$

by which the theorem is proved. □

A linear programming problem has a solution if ω_{max} (ω_{min}) has a value on the set Γ_P of permissible solutions. The linear programming problem has no solution if the system is unequal (1.5.0. 1) has no non-negative solutions or if the value ω_{max} (ω_{min}) does not have a finite value.

Constraints (1.5.0. 1) define in a k -dimensional space a convex domain Γ_P bounded by a set of hyperlevels

$$\sum_{j=1}^{k} \alpha_{ij} y_j = \beta_i, \text{ß} = 1, \ldots, m.$$

Let's call this area a Γ_P polyhedron, though in some cases, it can be endless. This area is called the *allowable solution area.* As the functions to be maximized or minimized are linear, classic mathematical methods by maxima or minima goal functions $\omega(y) = \omega(y_1, \ldots, y_k)$

reach at area boundaries Γ_P specified by the given restrictions. If the hyperlink $\omega(y) = \text{const}$ is not parallel to any of the hyperlinks mentioned, which represent the polyhedron, then the target function $\omega(y)$ will reach its maximum (minimum) in one of the tops of the polyhedron.

Let $A = [\alpha_{ij}]_{m \times k}$ be a data matrix with types $V_1, \ldots, V_m$, let $\beta \in \mathbb{R}^m$ and $\gamma \in \mathbb{R}^k$ be given vectors and let $y \in \mathbb{R}^k$ be an unknown vector. In *matrix form* problem (1.5.0. 1)–(1.5.0. 2) can be written as follows:

$$
\begin{aligned}
\min \quad & \gamma^T x, \\
\text{subj.} \quad & V_i^T x \leq \beta_i, \quad i \in I_1, \\
& V_i^T x = \beta_i, \quad i \in I_2, \\
& V_i^T x \geq \beta_i, \quad i \in I_3, \\
& y_j \geq 0, \qquad j \in J \subseteq \{1, \ldots, k\},
\end{aligned}
\tag{1.5.0. 3}
$$

where $I_1 \cup I_2 \cup I_3 = \{1, \ldots, m\}$, $I_1 \cap I_2 = \emptyset$, $I_1 \cap I_3 = \emptyset$, $I_2 \cap I_3 = \emptyset$.

If it's $I_2 = \{1, \ldots, m\}$ i $J = \{1, \ldots, k\}$, $A = [\alpha_{ij}]_{m \times n}$, $\gamma, y \in \mathbb{R}^n$, problem (1.5.0. 3) it comes down to the so called *standard format* linear programming problems

$$
\begin{aligned}
\min \quad & \gamma^T x, \\
\text{subj.} \quad & Ay = \beta, \\
& y \geq 0.
\end{aligned}
\tag{1.5.0. 4}
$$

In case $I_3 = \{1,\ldots,m\}$ and $J = \{1,\ldots,k\}$ problem (1.5.0. 3) it comes down to the so called *symmetric shape*

$$\min \quad \gamma^T x,$$
$$\text{subj.} \quad Ay \geq \beta, \qquad\qquad (1.5.0.\ 5)$$
$$y \geq 0.$$

Without destroying the general one can assume that $\beta_i \geq$ *is* 0 for every $i = 1,\ldots,m$ (otherwise, the corresponding inequality can be multiplied by -1).

For a vector y that satisfies the conditions (1.5.0. 1) we say yes is the *acceptable solution* to the problem. The admissible solution y^* is*minimum* if:

$$\gamma^T x^* \leq \gamma^T x$$

for each admissible solution y.

The problem given in the general form (1.5.0. 1)–(1.5.0. 2) can be transformed in standard or symmetrical form. If new unknowns are introduced:

$$y_{k+i} = \beta_i - \sum_{j=1}^{k} a_{ij}y_j, \quad i \in I_1$$

$$y_{k+i} = \sum_{j=1}^{k} a_{ij}y_j - \beta_i, \quad i \in I_3.$$

Then the conditions (1.5.0. 1) pass into the system of equations with $k + q = n$ unknown, where $q = |I_1| + |I_3|$.

$$\sum_{j=1}^{k} a_{ij} y_j + y_{k+i} = \beta_i, \quad i \in I_1$$

$$\sum_{j=1}^{k} a_{ij} y_j = \beta_i, \quad i \in I_2 \qquad (1.5.0.\ 6)$$

$$\sum_{j=1}^{k} a_{ij} y_j - y_{k+i} = \beta_i, \quad i \in I_3.$$

In doing so, we look at function

$$\omega = \gamma_1 y_1 + \cdots + \gamma_k x_k + \cdots + \gamma_n x_n \qquad (1.5.0.\ 7)$$

where $\gamma_{k+1} = \ldots = \gamma_n = 0$.

The following table illustrates the relationship between the basic forms of a linear problem.

Restriction	Canonical Form	Standard Form
$\alpha_i^T y \leq \beta_i$	$-\alpha_i^T y \geq -\beta_i$	$\alpha_i^T y + s_i = \beta_i, s_i \geq 0$
$\alpha_i^T y \geq \beta_i$		$\alpha_i^T y - s_i = \beta_i, s_i \geq 0$
$\alpha_i^T y = \beta_i$	$\alpha_i^T y \geq \beta_i, -\alpha_i^T y \geq -\beta_i$	

The s_i variables are called *slack variables* . Introducing each slack variable increases the dimension of problem n by 1, and the matrix A is expanded by the column of the unit matrix I, while the vector of the objective function γ is expanded by a null element. Variables from set $\{1, \ldots, n\} \backslash J$, not imposed the condition of non-negativity is called *free variables* . Each free variable $y_j, j \in \{1, \ldots, n\} \backslash J$ we can replace in the target function and all constraints with an expression

$y_j^+ - y_j^-$, with $y_j^+ \geq 0, y_j^- \geq 0$, and so we come to the model where all the variables are imposed a non-negativity condition. The problem thus posed is equivalent to the problem (1.5.0. 1)–(1.5.0. 2).

Example 1.5.1. Let us consider the problem of linear programming:

$$\begin{aligned} \min \quad & 5y_1 - 4y_2, \\ \text{subj.} \quad & y_1 + y_2 \leq 80, \\ & 3y_1 + y_2 \leq 180, \\ & y_1 + 3y_2 \leq 180, \\ & y_1 \geq 0, y_2 \geq 0. \end{aligned}$$

The standard form of this problem is obtained by introducing equalization y_3, y_4 and y_5 variables:

$$\begin{aligned} \min \quad & -5y_1 - 4y_2, \\ \text{subj.} \quad & y_1 + y_2 + y3 + y4 + y5 = 80, \\ & 3y_1 + y_2 + y3 + y4 + y5 = 180, \\ & y_1 + 3y_2 + y3 + y4 + y5 = 180, \\ & y_i \geq 0, \text{ß} = 1, \ldots, 5. \end{aligned}$$

To translate the problem in a general form to a symmetrical form equation type constraints need to be eliminated. Equations $V_i^T x = \beta_i$, and $\in I_2$ can be equivalently replaced by inequalities $V_i^T x \geq \beta_i$, $(-V_i)^T x \geq -\beta_i$, i and I_2. Limiting the form $(-V_i)^T x \geq -\beta_i$ is obtained by multiplying the shape constraint $V_i^T x \leq \beta_i$ with -1. Further, each free variable $y_j, j \in \{1, \ldots, n\} \backslash J$ replace in target function and all constraints as before with two non-negative variables each and thus we get a problem of type (1.5.0. 5).

Remark 1.5.1. *Considered to be a symmetrical vase assuming that the system of equations* $\{J_i\}_{i\in I_2}$ *is consistent and of complete rank. Otherwise, the first equations should be eliminated (for example, by the Gaussian method of elimination), that is, to form an equivalent system of full rank.*

From these considerations, it follows that one does not lose sight of what is observed in the linear problem of form (1.5.0. 4) or (1.5.0. 5). We mainly deal with the following linear programming problem in standard form because best suited for theoretical considerations.

The setting of the linear programming task in standard format is given as follows. The system of equations $Ay = \beta$ has a solution if the matrix rank of the system is equation:

$$A = \begin{bmatrix} \alpha_{11} & \alpha_{12} & \cdots & \alpha_{1n} \\ \vdots & \vdots & \ddots & \vdots \\ \alpha_{m1} & \alpha_{m2} & \cdots & \alpha_{mn} \end{bmatrix}$$

equal to the rank of the expanded matrix $[A|\beta]$, which is obtained by adding free member columns $\beta_1, \ldots, \beta_m$ matrix A (Kronecker-Capelli theorem). The rank r of the matrix A is called the rank of the system and represents the number of linearly independent equations between given constraints. If this condition is not met, the set of admissible solutions Γ_P is empty, and the problem has no solution.

Obviously, the rank of the system equation $Ay = \beta$ cannot be greater than the number of equations m, that is, is always filled by $r \leq m$, but the number r cannot be greater than the number of variables n, so it is also valid $r \leq n$. If $r < m$, then by applying the Gaussian algorithm, we reach a conclusion about system inconsistencies or eliminate $m - r$ related equations in $Ay = \beta$. So, suppose

$r = m$, i.e., that there are no constraints (1.5.0. 4) linearly dependent and that the system $Ay = \beta$ agrees. In the event that $r = m = n$, the system has a unique solution $y = A^{-1}\beta$ so it only remains to check the condition $y \geq 0$. We will be interested in the case $r = m < n$, when the number is linearly independent an equation smaller than the number of variables. Then, if the system equation $Ay = \beta$ agrees, it exists endless many solutions. Each of these solutions is obtained in the same way arbitrary values are selected for $n - r = s$ variables and then values are selected the remaining r variables are calculated from the system of equations $Ay = \beta$. The variables we calculate are called *dependent* or *basic* (there are r), and the variable sizes are arbitrarily called *independent* or *free* variables ($n - r = s$). Practically, from the system of equations r dependent variables expresses by possible $n - r = s$ independent variables, so arbitrary values are chosen for independent variables. As there are infinitely many independent variables to choose from of different values, the system of equations $Ay = \beta$ is infinite many solutions.

Definition 1.5.1. *A non-negative solution, obtained by applying independent values to be equal to zero, is called basic solution linear programming task.*

Example 1.5.2. The factory produces two types of items α_1 and α_2, both on machines M_1 and M_2. For α_1, M_1 is 2^h, M_2 for 4^h, and for type α_2, M_1 runs 4^h, and M_2 runs 2^h. The factory gets 3500 dinars per unit of product α_1, a 4800 per item α_2. How much to produce α_1 and α_2 items and how to use the work of M_1 and M_2 to maximize the daily profit of the factory?

Solution: Let y_1 be the number of items produced α_1 and y_2 the number of items produced α_2 items throughout the day. Then the daily profit of the factory is:

$$\omega(y) = 3500y_1 + 4800y_2$$

with conditions:

$$2y_1 + 4y_2 \leq 24$$
$$4y_1 + 2y_2 \leq 24$$
$$y_1 \geq 0, y_2 \geq 0.$$

This gave us a symmetrical shape. If we now introduce the slack variables y_3 and y_4 we get equivalent problem in standard format:

$$\max \quad 3500y_1 + 4800y_2$$
$$\text{subj.} \quad 2y_1 + 4y_2 - 24 = -y_3$$
$$4y_1 + 2y_2 - 24 = -y_4$$
$$y_1 \geq 0, y_2 \geq 0.$$

that is, in matrix form (1.5.0. 4):

$$A = \begin{bmatrix} 2 & 4 & 1 & 0 \\ 4 & 2 & 0 & 1 \end{bmatrix} \quad \beta = \begin{bmatrix} 24 \\ 24 \end{bmatrix} \quad \gamma = \begin{bmatrix} 3500 \\ 4800 \end{bmatrix}$$

1.6 Properties of a Set of Constraints

Let the linear programming problem be given in the standard format (1.5.0. 4). The set $\Gamma_P = \{y | Ay = \beta, y \geq 0\}$ on which the function ω is essentially defined influences extreme values and has interesting geometric properties. Below, we assume that $r = m < n$, where m and n are dimensions matrix A, and r is its rank. Then the system has infinitely many solutions so it makes sense to seek extreme value functions $\omega(y)$ defined on the set Γ_P. Label the columns of the matrix A as $K_1, \ldots, K_n$.

Note that the vectors $K_1, \ldots, K_n$, and β are dimensions of m.

Recall that the vectors $y_1, \ldots, y_n$ are linearly independent if it follows from the equation $\alpha_1 y_1 + \cdots + \alpha_n y_n = 0$ $\alpha_1 = \cdots = \alpha_n = 0$, otherwise they are linearly dependent. Form expression $a = \sigma a^1 + (1 - \sigma)a^2$, $0 \le \sigma \le 1$ is called the convex combination of vectors a^1 and a^2. Generally a convex combination of vectors $a^1, \ldots, a^k$ is any vector of a forms:

$$a = \sum_{i=1}^{k} \sigma_i a^i, \quad \sum_{i=1}^{k} \sigma_i = 1, \quad (\sigma_1, \ldots, \sigma_k \ge 0.)$$

The set of vectors K is convex if:

$$(\forall a^1, a^2 \in K)(\sigma a^1 + (1 - \sigma)a^2 \in K, \quad 0 \le \sigma \le 1).$$

Geometrically, the set K is convex if for every two points $a^1, a^2 \in K$ implies that the segment defined by these points is contained in K. The smallest convex set in $\mathbb{R}^n$ contains $n + 1$ of different points is called *simplex* in $\mathbb{R}^n$; in space $\mathbb{R}^2$ each triangle is simplex, and in $\mathbb{R}^3$ each tetrahedron is simplex. Here are some well-known statements and basic definitions that are necessary for studying simplex methods as well as internal methods dots.

Theorem 1.6.1. *The set $\Gamma_P = \{y | Ay = \beta, y \ge 0\}$ is convex.*

Proof. Let be $y^1, y^2 \in \Gamma_P$. Then for their convex combination

$$y = \sigma y^1 + (1 - \sigma)y^2, \quad 0 \le \sigma \le 1$$

we have that

$$Ay = \sigma Ay^1 + (1 - \sigma)Ay^2 = \sigma\beta + \beta - \sigma\beta = \beta.$$

How obvious $y \geq 0$, it is $y \in \Gamma_P$. □

Definition 1.6.1. *A possible solution to y isosnovno (bazicno) if they are in the equation:*

$$\beta = y_1 K_1 + \cdots + y_n K_n$$

vectors K_i for which $y_i > 0$, are linearly independent.

Note that the basic solution may have the most m coordinate greater than zero.

Definition 1.6.2. *A basic solution for which it is true A m coordinate greater than zero is called undegenerated. Basic a solution for which less than m coordinates is greater than zero is called degenerate.*

Note that from n columns of matrix A, i.e., of vectors $K_1, \ldots, K_n$ we can form $\binom{n}{m}$ submatrices with m columns. If the vectors $K_{i_1}, \ldots, K_{i_m}$ are linearly independent, then matrix $\beta = [K_{i_1} \cdots K_{i_m}]$ regular and there is β^{-1}. Then it is vector $y = \beta^{-1}\beta$ uniquely determined and if $y \geq is$, then y is the basic solution. Note that $y \in \mathbb{R}^n$ a $\beta^{-1}\beta \in \mathbb{R}^m$, and that $y = \beta^{-1}\beta$ by definition means that the coordinates are y_i for *and* $\notin \{i_1, \ldots, i_m\}$ equal to zero.

Definition 1.6.3. *The matrix $\alpha_\beta = [K_{i_1} \cdots K_{i_m}]$ isbasic (basic) if regular. The remaining columns of the A matrix form the nonbasic matrix α_N. The variables $y_{i_1}, \ldots y_{i_m}$ are called basic while the remaining variables we call non-base . Two basic matrices are adjacent if they differ in one column.*

Let α_β be a basis matrix. Now the system from (1.5.0. 4) can be written as:

$$\alpha_B x_\beta + \alpha_N x_N = \beta \implies y_\beta = \alpha_\beta^{-1}\beta - \alpha_\beta^{-1}\alpha_N x_N$$

If we now put $y_N = 0$ we get one basic solution $(y = (y_\beta, y_N) = (\beta^{-1}\beta, 0)$, after the corresponding renumbering variables). On the contrary, each basic solution determines the corresponding basic matrix (if under generated, then is this matrix unique and otherwise not). This justifies the name "basic matrix" in the Definition 1.6.3.

It follows from the previous definition that the maximum number of basic solutions is equal to $\binom{n}{m}$.

Definition 1.6.4. *The point y is the extreme point of the convex set Γ_P if it satisfies the conditions*

$$y = \sigma y^{(1)} + (1 - \sigma)y^{(2)} \wedge \sigma \in [0, 1] \Leftrightarrow y = y^{(1)} = y^{(2)}.$$

Definition 1.6.5. *The basic solution of y system $Ay = \beta$ for which condition $y \geq 0$ is also true basic admissible solution.*

Example 1.6.1. In the example (1.5.1) there is:

$$K_1 = \begin{bmatrix} 1 \\ 3 \\ 1 \end{bmatrix}, \quad K_2 = \begin{bmatrix} 1 \\ 1 \\ 3 \end{bmatrix}, \quad K_3 = \begin{bmatrix} 1 \\ 0 \\ 0 \end{bmatrix}, \quad K_4 = \begin{bmatrix} 0 \\ 1 \\ 0 \end{bmatrix}, \quad K_5 = \begin{bmatrix} 0 \\ 0 \\ 1 \end{bmatrix}.$$

Since $m = 3$ and $n = 5$, are basic matrices and basic solutions has at most 10. Determine basic matrices, basic solutions and values of the objective function in them:

$$\beta_1 = [K_3\,K_4\,K_5], \quad y^1 = (0,0,80,180,180), \quad \omega^1 = 0,$$
$$\beta_2 = [K_1\,K_3\,K_5], \quad y^2 = (60,0,20,0,120), \quad \omega^2 = -300,$$
$$\beta_3 = [K_1\,K_1\,K_5], \quad y^3 = (50,30,0,0,40), \quad \omega^3 = -370,$$
$$\beta_4 = [K_1\,K_2\,K_4], \quad y^4 = (30,50,0,40,0), \quad \omega^4 = -350,$$
$$\beta_5 = [K_2\,K_3\,K_4], \quad y^5 = (0,60,20,120,0), \quad \omega^1 = -240.$$

So there are five basic solutions. The following solutions are not permissible for other databases:

$$\beta_6 = [K_1\,K_2\,K_3], \quad y^6 = (45,45,-10,0,0), \quad \omega^6 = -405,$$
$$\beta_7 = [K_1\,K_4\,K_5], \quad y^7 = (80,0,0,-60,100), \quad \omega^7 = -400,$$
$$\beta_8 = [K_1\,K_3\,K_4], \quad y^8 = (180,0,-100,-360,0), \quad \omega^8 = -900,$$
$$\beta_9 = [K_2\,K_3\,K_5], \quad y^9 = (0,180,-100,0,-360), \quad \omega^9 = -720,$$
$$\beta_{10} = [K_2\,K_4\,K_5], \quad y^{10} = (0,80,0,100,-60), \quad \omega^{10} = -320.$$

A very important fact is the existence of a basic solution follows from the existence of an admissible solution, which follows from the following theorem.

Theorem 1.6.2. *If* $\Gamma_P = \{y\,|\,Ay = \beta, y \geq 0\} \neq \emptyset$, *then it contains at least one basic solution.*

Proof. Suppose $y = (y_1, \ldots, y_n) \in \Gamma_P$ is valid. If necessary we renumber the columns K_i and the coordinates of the vector y such that $y_i > 0$ for $i \leq p$ i $y_i = 0$ for $i > p$. Now it is valid

$$\beta = \sum_{i=1}^{n} x_i K_i = \sum_{i=1}^{p} x_i K_i.$$

If the vectors $K_1, \ldots, K_p$ are linearly independent, then $p \leq m$ and y is the basic solution. If the vectors $K_1, \ldots, K_p$ are linearly dependent, then they exist $\sigma_1, \ldots, \sigma_p \in \mathbb{R}$ such that

$$\sum_{i=1}^{p} \sigma_i K_i = 0$$

and then exists $\sigma_i \neq 0$, $1 \leq i \leq p$. Let $\sigma_k \neq 0$ be and $\sigma_k > 0$. Then:

$$K_k = -\sum_{j \neq k} \frac{\sigma_j}{\sigma_k} K_j \quad \text{i} \quad \beta = \sum_{j \neq k} \left(y_j - y_k \frac{\sigma_j}{\sigma_k} \right) K_j.$$

Thus, the vector β is represented as the sum of $p - 1$ columns of the matrix A. If moreover, $y_j - y_k \frac{\sigma_j}{\sigma_k} \geq 0$, $j \neq k$, then the vector:

$$\begin{aligned}
y^1 &= (y_1 - y_k \frac{\sigma_1}{\sigma_k}, \ldots, y_{k-1} - y_k \frac{\sigma_{k-1}}{\sigma_k}, 0, \\
&\quad y_{k+1} - y_k \frac{\sigma_{k+1}}{\sigma_k}, 0, \ldots, 0, y_p - y_k \frac{\sigma_p}{\sigma_k}, 0, \ldots, 0)
\end{aligned}$$

Element of the set Γ_P (i.e., the solution of $Ay = \beta$). If it is $\sigma_j \leq 0$, then obviously $y_j^1 \geq 0$. Otherwise $y_j^1 = y_j - y_k \frac{\sigma_j}{\sigma_k} \geq 0$, which is equivalent to $\frac{y_j}{\sigma_j} \geq \frac{y_k}{\sigma_k}$. Therefore, in this case, too, $y_j^1 \geq 0$, so we conclude that $y_1 \Gamma_P$. However, y^1 has at most $p - 1$ strictly positive coordinates, which is a contradiction. Therefore, the vectors $K_1, \ldots, K_p$ are linearly independent, and y is a basic admissible solution. $\square$

The link between the basic solutions and the top set Γ_P is given by the following theorem.

Theorem 1.6.3. *If $y \in \Gamma_P$ is the basic solution of the system $Ay = \beta$, $y \geq 0$, then y is the extreme point of the set Γ_P. Conversely, if it is y is the extreme point of Γ_P, then y is the basic solution.*

Proof. Let y be a basic solution and let it be a new numbering (if necessary)

$$\beta = \sum_{j=1}^{m} x_j K_j, \quad y = (y_1, \ldots, y_m, 0, \ldots, 0).$$

Suppose y is not an extreme point of the set Γ_P,, i.e., since $y^1, y^2 \in \Gamma_P$, $y^1 = (y_1^1, \ldots, y_n^1), y^2 = (y_1^2, \ldots, y_n^2)$, such that:

$$y = \sigma y^1 + (1 - \sigma) y^2, \quad 0 < \sigma < 1.$$

How it is $y_i = \sigma y_i^1 + (1 - \sigma) y_i^2$, $i = 1, \ldots, n$, then $y_i^1 = y_i^2 = 0$ for $i > m$. Therefore, y^1 i y^2 are basic solutions for the base $K_1, \ldots, K_m$,.

$$\beta = \sum_{j=1}^{m} x_j^1 K_j = \sum_{j=1}^{m} x_j^2 K_j = \sum_{j=1}^{m} x_j K_j.$$

Since $K_1, \ldots, K_m$ are linearly independent, this is $y = y^1 = y^2$ which means that y is an extreme point of the set Γ_P.

Let us prove the opposite. Let $y\Gamma_P$ be the extreme point of Γ_P. New by numbering (if necessary) we obtain that $y_i > 0$ for $i \leq p$ i $y_i = 0$ for $i \geq p$. Suppose that the corresponding vectors $K_1, \ldots, K_m$ from $\beta = \sum_{j=1}^{p} x_j K_j$, linearly dependent, i.e., Yes there is at least one $\sigma_j > 0$, $1 \leq j \leq p$, so it applies:

$$\sum_{j=1}^{p} \sigma_j K_j = 0.$$

Now we have:

$$\beta = \sum_{j=1}^{p} x_j K_j \pm \sum_{j=1}^{p} \mu \sigma_j K_j = \sum_{j=1}^{p} (y_j \pm \mu \sigma_j) K_j$$

for each $\mu \in \mathbb{R}$. If $\mu = \frac{1}{2} \min \left\{ \frac{y_j}{\sigma_j} \mid 1 \leq j \leq p \right\}$, then $y_j \pm \mu \sigma_j > 0$, $1 \leq j \leq p$, so

$$
\begin{aligned}
y^1 &= (y_1 + \mu \sigma_1, \ldots, y_p + \mu \sigma_p, 0, \ldots, 0) \in \Gamma_P, \\
y^2 &= (y_1 - \mu \sigma_1, \ldots, y_p - \mu \sigma_p, 0, \ldots, 0) \in \Gamma_P,
\end{aligned}
$$

and it is valid

$$
y = \frac{1}{2} y^1 + \frac{1}{2} y^2,
$$

which is impossible because y is an extreme point expensive Γ_P. □

It follows from the foregoing that the number of extreme points is less than $\binom{n}{m}$.

Corollary 1.6.1. *The set Γ_P finally has many extreme points*

Proof. Each basic matrix β determines exactly one basic solution (by Theorem 1.6.3), and for any basic solution it can find the corresponding matrix β such that Theorem 1.6.3 holds. We conclude that the basis matrices have no less than the basic solutions, and, based on the previous theorem of extreme points, the set Γ_P. Obviously, the basis matrices have no more than a binomial coefficient of n over m. □

The significance of the previous theorem and the consequence is that the number of potential extrema reduces $\omega(y)$ functions from (in the general case) an infinite set Γ_P to a finite set of vertices that has a maximum of the binomial coefficient of n over m elements. The objective function $\omega(y)$ will be the maximum or minimum in the foundations of the convex set Γ_p. Formally, it is sufficient to calculate the values of the objective function in all extreme points of the set Γ_P and determine that point, or points, in which the value of the function $\omega(y)$ is extreme. This number of potential extremes grows rapidly with an increasing value of m i n.

Example 1.6.2. We look at the following problem

$$\begin{aligned} \max \quad & \omega(y) = 2y_1 + 5y_2 \\ \text{subj.} \quad & y_1 + 4y_2 \le 24, \; 3y_1 + y_2 \le 21, y_1 + y_2 \le 9. \end{aligned}$$

After calculating the values of $\omega(A), \omega(B), \omega(C), \omega(D)$, we can see that the maximum value has $\omega(B) = \omega(4,5) = 33$, which is the solution to the problem.

We will prove later in Theorem 2.1.1 that the extremum of the function $\omega(y)$ (if any) is exactly at the extremes of the set Γ_P, and by Theorem 1.6.3 in the admissible solutions of $Ay = \beta$.

The following theorem provides the criterion for detecting the boundlessness of the set Γ_P.

Theorem 1.6.4. *If there is a basic matrix* $\alpha_B = [K_{i_1} \cdots K_{i_m}]$ *and the column* K_p *of the matrix* A *such that* $\alpha_B^{-1} K_p \le 0$, *then* Γ_P *is an unlimited set.*

Proof. Let $\alpha_B = [K_1 \dots K_m]$ i $B^{-1}K_p \le 0$ be valid for each p. Then:

$$K_p = \sigma_1 K_1 + \cdots + \sigma_m K_m$$

and it is true $\sigma_j \le 0$, $1 \le j \le m$. Now it is:

$$\beta = \sum_{j=1}^{m} x_j K_j - \mu K_p + \mu K_p, \quad \mu > 0,$$

follows:

$$\beta = \sum_{j=1}^{m}(y_j - \mu\sigma_j)K_j + \mu K_p, \quad \mu > 0,$$

where's he from:

$$y^\mu = (y_1 - \mu\sigma_1, \ldots, y_m - \mu\sigma_m, 0, \ldots, 0, \overset{(p)}{\rightarrow} \mu, 0, \ldots, 0) \in \Gamma_P$$

for each $\mu > 0$, Γ_P is an unlimited set. ☐

If for every basic matrix β and every vector K_p vector $\beta^{-1}K_p$ negative then the set Γ_P is limited and each $y\Gamma_P$ is a convex combination of basic (basic) solutions. So, it is enough to know only basic solutions. If one basic solution is known, we can determine another basic solution. Let $\beta = [K_1 \cdots K_m]$ be basic matrix and let $y = \beta^{-1}\beta = (y_1, \ldots, y_m, 0, \ldots, 0)$ known basic the solution. If $\beta^{-1}K_r \le 0$ for K_r, set Γ_P is unlimited so suppose Γ_P is restricted, i.e., $\beta^{-1}K_r$ nonnegative. Let it be:

$$\beta^{-1}K_r = (\sigma_1, \ldots, \sigma_m, 0, \ldots, 0)$$

non-negative and let it be $\sigma_k > 0$ for some $k, 1 \le k \le m$. Then from:

$$K_r = \sigma_1 K_1 + \cdots + \sigma_m K_m$$

follows:

$$K_k = \frac{1}{\sigma_k}K_r - \sum_{j \neq k}\frac{\sigma_j}{\sigma_k}K_j. \tag{1.6.0.1}$$

By replacement (1.6.0.1) u

$$\beta = y_1 K_1 + \cdots + y_k K_k + \cdots + y_m K_m$$

we get:

$$\beta = y_1 K_1 + \cdots + \frac{y_k}{\sigma_k} K_r - \sum_{j \neq k} y_k \frac{\sigma_j}{\sigma_k} K_j + \cdots + y_m K_m$$

to jest

$$\beta = \sum_{j \neq k} (y_j - y_k \frac{\sigma_j}{\sigma_k}) K_j + \frac{y_k}{\sigma_k} K_r.$$

An appropriate solution

$$y^1 = (y_1 - y_k \frac{\sigma_1}{\sigma_k}, \ldots, \overset{(k)}{\to} 0, \ldots, y_m - y_k \frac{\sigma_m}{\sigma_k}, 0, \ldots, 0, \overset{(r)}{\to} \frac{y_k}{\sigma_k}, 0, \ldots, 0)$$

is in the set Γ_P if $y_j - y_k \frac{\sigma_j}{\sigma_k} \geq 0, j \neq k$, hundred is filled if k is chosen so that:

$$\frac{y_k}{\sigma_k} = \min_j \left\{ \frac{y_j}{\sigma_j} | sigma_j > 0 \right\}.$$

The base solution y^1 is different from y if $y_k > 0$ which is fulfilled if y is a non-degenerate solution. The corresponding basic matrix is obtained by replacing column K_k with column K_r.

1.7   Geometrical Method

It corresponds to each condition of negativity in vector space $\mathbb{R}^n$ half-space in which the corresponding variable is non-negative. Each conditional equation in $\mathbb{R}^n$ corresponds to one hyper-straight. Each conditional inequality corresponds to the half-space bounded hyperbolic associated with the corresponding equation. A set of all the admissible vectors y is the intersection of all given half-spaces and given hypergraphs, therefore, constitutes a convex polyhedron Γ_P. The equation $\gamma^T x = k$ for some k is a hyperparallel parallel to space $\mathbb{R}^{n-1}$ which is normal at γ. Projection of polyhedra Γ_P on the direction determined by the vector γ is a closed set of $[l, \Lambda]$ real numbers, where l minimum and Λ maximum of the objective function (1.5.0. 2). Appropriately hyper straight normal to γ are touched by hyper straight polyhedra Γ_P. The common points of these touching hyper-lines with the polyhedron Γ_P give values in which the function (1.5.0. 2) reaches an extreme value.

The geometric method can be used for problems containing $n = 2$ pro men li ve, and the highest š is $n = 3$ pro men li ve. The linear programming task is given in the basic form it fulfills the condition $n - m = 2$ (and the highest $n - m = 3$) can also be to geometric geometry. The geometric method, while not very basic, is used because easy access to the general algebraic method.

Let be given a linear problem in form:

$$\max \omega(y) = \gamma_1 y_1 + \ldots + \gamma_n y_n$$

$$\text{subj. } \alpha_{11} y_1 + \alpha_{12} y_2 + \ldots + \alpha_{1n} y_n \leq \beta_1$$

$$\ldots\ldots\ldots$$

$$\alpha_{m1} y_1 + \alpha_{m2} y_2 + \ldots + \alpha_{mn} y_n \leq \beta_m.$$

For a given system we know that every solution of the system is an unequal solution one point space $\mathbb{R}^n$, and a set of nonnegative admissible ones Γ_p is a subset of $\mathbb{R}^n$. Each of the unequal acts:

$$\sum_{j=1}^{n} \alpha_{ij} y_j \leq \beta_i, \text{ß} = 1, 2, \ldots, m$$

specifies a subset of $D_i \subset \mathbb{R}^n$, $i = 1, \ldots, m$ representing the set of ta aka on the one hand hyper-straight:

$$\sum_{j=1}^{n} \alpha_{ij} y_j = \beta_i,$$

So, the area of admissible solutions (polyhedron in $\mathbb{R}^n$) is determined by the intersection of sets:

$$\Gamma_p = D_1 \cap D_2 \cap \cdots \cap D_m \cap D_{m+1} \cap \cdots \cap D_{m+n},$$

where subsets $D_{m+1}, \ldots, D_{m+n}$ are obtained from the conditions of the nonnegativity of the variables $y_1 \geq 0, \ldots, y_n \geq 0$. The set of admissible solutions geometrically represents the polyhedron (simplification complex).

The set of points where the function of goal $\omega(y)$ has the value d also represents one hyperline $\mathcal{W}_{\omega,d} = \{y \in \mathbb{R}^n \| \omega(y) = d\}$, which, depending on the value of d, we can translate in the direction of the vector γ. Now the problem of linear programming comes down to finding it maximum (minimum) values for d such that $\mathcal{W}_{\omega,d} \cap \Gamma_P \neq \emptyset$. It is on this fact that the geometric method is based. It is now clear why this method is applicable only in the cases $n = 2$ and $n = 3$. Note also that, by theorem 2.1.1, the extremum goal functions reach at the extreme point of the set Γ_P. The set of optimal points Γ_P^* from the same theorem is convex and represents a k -dimensional polyhedron. The objective function, which for $\omega(y) = d$ is interpreted as hyper-straight, reaching the maximum (minimum) in one vertex of the polyhedron (single unique optimal solution) or one by one polyhedra if the hyperline $\omega(y) = d$ is parallel to it (the case of infinite but many optimal solutions).

This model consists of a function $\omega(y)$ and a constraint (system non-uniform), and is called the mathematical model. Factory daily profit is a function of $\omega(y)$ that depends on two variables y_1 and y_2, and this form of dependency is linear. Indeed, value units of α_1 in the market, i.e., 3500 is multiplied by the number units of y_1 of that type of product produced, and to that added the unit value of the product α_2, 4800 multiplied by the number y_2 produced the only α_2 items. The limitations stem from the fact that M_1 produces a unit of product α_1 for 2^h. Hence the linear ones unequal in the above mathematical model, where the first refers to options are M_1 and the other is options M_2. These inequalities add to the nature of the variables sought y_1 and y_2, which are to be nonnegative quantities. The set Γ_p is a convex set because it is the intersection of the finite number convex sets. The $\omega(y)$ function will suffice to be maximum or minimum in the tops of the convex set Γ_p.

If the boundary graphs are represented in the coordinate system $y_1 y_2$ yields one quadrilateral $ABCD$, which is convex, in area of which there are possible solutions of a given linear model. Within the quadrilateral, as well as at the points of the edge, (AB, BC, CD, and DA) there are possible solutions to a given model. However, it is noted that $C(4,4)$ with $y_1 = 4$ and $y_2 = 4$ such that it corresponds to the optimal solution of a given model, because it is farthest from the real $3500y_1 + 4800y_2 = 0$ received from the function targets $\omega(y)$ for $\omega(y) = 0$. Indeed, the corresponding value of the criterion function is $\max \omega(y) = 3500 * 4 + 4800 * 4 = 14000 + 19200 = 33200$ dinars daily profit, which is the highest possible under the given conditions.

Example 1.7.1. Two mines R_1 and R_2 supply coal to the three cities A, B and C. The R_1 mine can deliver 500 tons of coal a day, and mine R_2 800 tons. Cost of transporting 1 tonne of coal to new units from mines to cities are shown in the table. How to arrange transportation to minimize the total cost of transportation?

Mines	A	B	C
R_1	8	5	5
R_2	4	6	8

Re š: Mark with y_1 the number of tons of coal to be mined R_1 to the city A, and with y_2 the number of tons of coal from R_1 to B. Considering that in cities the daily demand is the same as much coal as we can get from the mine a day, we can other quantities of coal to express by y_1 and y_2:

$$R_1 \rightarrow C : 500 - y_1 - y_2$$
$$R_2 \rightarrow A : 500 - y_1$$
$$R_2 \rightarrow B : 400 - y_2$$
$$R_2 \rightarrow C : 800 - 500 + y_1 - 400 + y_2 = y_1 + y_2 - 100.$$

Restrictions and conditions of non-negativity are:

$$(D_1) \quad 500 - y_1 - y_2 \geq 0$$

$Rightarrow y_1 + y_2 \leq 500$

$$(D_2) \quad 500 - y_1 \geq 0$$

$Rightarrow y_1 \leq 500$

$$(D_3) \quad 400 - y_2 \geq 0$$

$Rightarrow y_2 \leq 400$

$$(D_4) \quad y_1 + y_2 - 100 \geq 0$$

$Rightarrow y_1 + y_2 \geq 100$

$$(D_5) \quad y_1 \geq 0$$

$$(D_6) \quad y_2 \geq 0.$$

The areas $D_1, D_2, \ldots, D_6$ are indicated by the arrows in the given image, and the area of permissible solutions:

$$D = \bigcap_{i=1}^{6} D_i$$

Total costs are:

$$\omega = 8y_1 + 5y_2 + 5(500 - y_1 - y_2) + 4(500 - y_1)$$
$$+ 6(400 - y_2) + 8(y_1 + y_2 - 100)$$
$$= 7y_1 + 2y_2 + 6500.$$

The quantities of y_1 and y_2 should now be determined so that the total costs are minimal. Real $7y_1 + 2y_2 + 6500 = $ const takes the smallest value in the points of the permissible values (D), which are nearest to the coordinate origin. For this reason, the simplest is to calculate the value the objective functions in the points of the permissible values of (D), which are closest to the coordinate origin. The simplest is because of this compute the value of the target function in points $M_4(100, 0)$ i $M_5(0, 100)$:

$$\omega(M_4) = 7 * 100 + 2 * 0 + 6500 = 7200$$

$$\omega(M_5) = 7 * 0 + 2 * 100 + 6500 = 6700 = \omega_{min}.$$

In this way, the minimum cost of transportation from R_1 and R_2 to the mine cities A, B and C are provided if the transportation plan is as follows ($y_1 = 0, y_2 = 100$):

Mines	A	B	C
R_1 (500)	0	100	400
R_2 (800)	500	300	0

In this table, therefore, the optimal coal transportation plan is shown. Like this, the task is known as the transport task. As we see it, in the case where we have two dispatch stations (mines) and three receiving stations (cities), the transport task can be solved geometrically, because the number of unknowns is reduced to two thanks to provided that the quantity of coal offered by the mine is R_1 i R_2 equals the amount of coal in cities A, B i C.

Example 1.7.2. Solve the problem of linear programming by the graphical method:

$$\max \quad \omega(y) = 2y_1 + 3y_2$$
$$\text{subj.} \quad y_1 + y_2 \leq 5$$
$$y_1 - 3y_2 \geq 0$$
$$2y_1 + 3y_2 \geq 6$$
$$y_i \geq 0, \quad i = 1, 2.$$

Mark we have restrictions and conditions of negativity respectively with D_1, D_2, D_3, D_4, D_5:

$$(D_1) \quad y_1 + y_2 \leq 5$$
$$(D_2) \quad y_1 - 3y_2 \geq 0$$

$$(D_3) \quad 2y_1 + 3y_2 \geq 6$$
$$(D_4) \quad y_1 \geq 0$$
$$(D_5) \quad y_2 \geq 0.$$

Each of the limitations and conditions of non-negativity is represented by in the space $\mathbb{R}^2$. Clearly, all permissible solutions will be found in a subset.

$$D = D_1 \cap D_2 \cap D_3 \cap D_4 \cap D_5.$$

Show the geometric area of permissible solutions determined by planes $D_i (i = 1, 2, ..., 6)$:

The refined surface represents the domain of permissible solutions. The optimal solution will be at one of the points A, B, C, D. Yes, to determine which point represents the optimal solution, we need to first draw a line representing the objective function for $\omega = 0$. The law thus drawn should be shifted in the direction of growth in parallel unknown y_1 and y_2 until we reach the last point š of the refined surface, or to the last point of the polygon permissible solutions. At this point, the target function will have the maximum value; i.e., this point will optimally represent the solution. In this case, this will apparently be that B is the coordinates that should be calculated and included in the objective function. From the system:

$$y_1 + y_2 = 5y_1 - 3y_2 \quad = 0$$

we get $B(15/4, 5/4)$ and

$$\omega_{max} = \omega(B) = \omega(15/4, 5/4) = 2 * 15/4 + 3 * 5/4 = 45/4.$$

Now we can draw the following conclusions regarding the geometric method:

I. The area of admissible solutions of D is at least one vertex at its boundary that represents the optimum solution. The proof follows from the theorem of Weierstrass, which says that a continuous the function given on a closed and bounded set reaches at least at one point in the set of the highest value, and at least at one point the smallest value. Since the objective function is linear and continuous, this theorem is valid when it comes to convex and bounded areas.

II. There is no linear programming task the optimal solution when the set of admissible solutions is D empty or when D is unbounded and at the same time the objective function, which is minimized (maximized), is infinite no decreases (grows).

III If two optimal solutions are obtained then they are all true between these points, optimal solutions. Thus, if $y^{(1)} \in D$ and $y^{(2)} \in D$ are optimal solutions, then each is a vector of shape:

$$y_\sigma^{(0)} = \sigma y^{(2)} + (1 - \sigma) y^{(1)}, \quad 0 \le \sigma \le 1$$

In the case of $n = 2$, if the constraints are represented graphically in the coordinate system $y_1 y_2$ a convex polygon is obtained, at its extremes (extreme points) find a possible solution to a given linear programming problem. Topics farthest from the real one determined by the goal function represents the optimal solution to a given problem.

The geometric method, for the case $n = 2$, we implemented in the programming language MATHEMATICA [67]. This is how the GEOM [56], program was created, which introduced a linear programming problem in symmetric form from the two variables find the optimal solution by the geometric method and graphically show all the intermediate steps. We used the following standard functions to graphically display the set of Γ_P allowable solutions MATHEMATICA programming language: `InequalityPlot`, `InequalitySolve`, `FindInstance`, etc. These features are in the standard packages `Graphics'InequalityGraphics` and `Algebra'InequalitySolve`. Complete code GEOM and implementation details are shown in the appendix and can be found in the work [56]. Let's now consider the work of GEOM in the following example:

Example 1.7.3. Solve linear programming problem:

$$\begin{aligned}
\max \quad & w(y,y) = 8y + 12y \\
subj. \quad & 8y + 4y \leq 600 \\
& 2y + 3y \leq 300 \\
& 4y + 3y \leq 360 \\
& 5y + 10y \geq 600 \\
& y - y \geq -80 \\
& y - y \leq 40 \\
& y, y \geq 0
\end{aligned}$$

We solve the problem with the following command:

```
Geom[8y+12y,{8y+4y< = 600, 2y+3y< = 300, 4y+3y< = 360,

5y+10y> = 600,y> = 0, y> = 0}]
```

The program gives a graphical representation of the set of admissible solutions Γ_P, as well as the right one corresponding to the objective function $(\mathcal{W}_{w,d})$. We move "upward" right, in the direction of the vector $\gamma = \begin{bmatrix} 8 \\ 12 \end{bmatrix}$, as long as there is a cross-section with the polygon of permissible solutions.

The program also provides the optimal solution (or an expression that describes all the optimal solutions). In this case, it is:

$$y^* = \sigma \begin{bmatrix} \frac{190}{3} \\ \frac{70}{3} \end{bmatrix} + (1 - \sigma) \begin{bmatrix} 45 \\ 60 \end{bmatrix}, 0 \leq \sigma \leq 1$$

Chapter 2

Simplex Method

The simplex method is based on three essential principles: (1) It is possible to determine at least one permissible solution (plan), which is often referred to as a baseline plan or a permissible baseline plan. (2) It is possible to check whether the basic allowable plan is optimal or not. (3) There is a possibility that in case the plan is not optimal, a new one can be selected, which is closer to the optimum.

According to the above, the simplex method is based on the successive improvement of the initial admissible plan until an optimal plan is obtained. The simplex algorithm method also allows one to determine whether a task is serious or not; or whether there is a contradiction in the restrictions.

2.1 Properties of Simplex Methods

Note first that the vector y^* in which the objective function $\omega(y)$ reaches extreme value need not be unique. The following theorem shows that the target function reaches an extreme value in some of the extreme points of the set Γ_P.

Theorem 2.1.1. *If* $\Gamma_P = \{y : Ay = \beta, y \geq 0\}$ *limited set i* $\omega(y) = \gamma_1 y_1 + \cdots + \gamma_n x_n$ *given a linear function, then there is a bar one extreme point* $y^* \in \Gamma_p$ *such that:*

$$\inf_{y \in \Gamma_P} \omega(y) = \omega(y^*).$$

Set $\{y \,|\, y \in \Gamma_P, \, \omega(y) = \omega(y^*)\}$ *is convex.*

Proof. Let $y^1, \ldots, y^p$ be the extreme points of the set Γ_P and let is y^* the extreme point for which $\omega(y^i) \geq \omega(y^*)$, $i = 1, \ldots, p$. How is each $y \in \Gamma_P$ a convex combination of extremes dots, there are positive scalars $\sigma_1, \ldots, \sigma_p$ such that it is:

$$y = \sum_{k=1}^{p} \sigma_k y^k, \quad \sum_{k=1}^{p} \sigma_k = 1.$$

Now we have:

$$\omega(y) = \omega\left(\sum_{k=1}^{p} \sigma_k y^k\right) = \sum_{k=1}^{p} \sigma_k \omega(y^k) \geq \sum_{k=1}^{p} \sigma_k \omega(y^*) = \omega(y^*),$$

which proves that ω reaches the minimum in y^*.

Let $\omega(y^1) = \omega(y^2) = \omega(y^*)$ be valid. Then:

$$\omega(\sigma y^1 + (1 - \sigma)y^2) = \sigma\omega(y^1) + (1 - \sigma)\omega(y^2) = \omega(y^*)$$

for each $0 \leq \sigma \leq 1$. $\square$

The significance of the previous theorem is that the number of potential extremes of $\omega(y)$ reduces from (in the general case) an infinite set Γ_P to a finite set of vertices that has a maximum of the binomial coefficient of n over m elements. Formally, it is sufficient to calculate the values of the objective function in all extreme points of the set Γ_P and determine that point, or points, in which the value of the function $\omega(y)$ is extreme.

Let $j_1 < \cdots < j_m$ be indexes such that $\mathcal{A}_B = \{K_{j_1}, \ldots, K_{j_m}\}$ one base of A and let $\beta = \{j_1, \ldots, j_m\}$. Unless otherwise emphasized, we imply that base $\mathcal{A}_B$ is joined by base submatrix $\alpha_B = [K_{j_1} \ldots K_{j_m}]$. If the basic solution is admissible, we call base $\mathcal{A}_B$ *admissible base*. Suppose:

$$N = \{i_1, \ldots, i_{n-m}\} = \{1, \ldots, n\}\backslash B$$

growing set and let $\alpha_N = \{K_{i_1}, \ldots, K_{i_{n-m}}\}$. Now the constraint system $Ay = \beta$ can be written in the form:

$$\alpha_B x_B + \alpha_N x_N = \beta, \qquad (2.1.0.1)$$

where y_B is the vector of the base and y_N the vector of the non-base variables. Now from (2.1.0.1) it follows $y_B = \alpha_B^{-1}\beta - \alpha_B^{-1}\alpha_N x_N$, so it can be eliminated basic variables from the target function. Analogous to y_B i y_N we define γ_B and γ_N such that:

$$\gamma^T x = \gamma_B^T x_B + \gamma_N^T x_N = \gamma_B^T A_B^{-1}\beta + (\gamma_N^\tau - \gamma_B^T A_B^{-1}\alpha_N)y_N,$$

hence $\gamma^T x^* = \gamma_B^T A_B^{-1}\beta$ for the base solution y^*. Let's introduce tags

$$d' = \gamma_B^T A_B^{-1}\beta, (\gamma_N')^\tau = \gamma_N^\tau - \gamma_B^T A_B^{-1}\alpha_N, \alpha_N' = \alpha_B^{-1}\alpha_N, \beta' = \alpha_B^{-1}\beta.$$

Now the standard form of the problem (1.5.0. 4) can be written in equivalent form:

$$\min \& d' + (\gamma'_N)^T x_N,$$
$$\text{subj.} \quad y_B \quad + \alpha'_N y_N = \beta', \quad (2.1.0.2)$$
$$y_B \quad \geq 0, \, y_N \geq 0.$$

Problem (2.1.0.1) is the *canonical form of problem* (1.5.0.4) *relative to base* α_B. In the canonical form, the matrices of the corresponding system are one řank with basic variables with hold different unit columns, and in the objective function the coefficients with the basic variables are equal to zero.

Lemma 2.1.1. *The vector of coefficients of the objective function in canonical the form of the problem of not ar s programming is uniquely determined base* $\alpha_B,$, *i.e., does not depend on the order of the columns in the matrix* $\mathcal{A}_B$.

Proof. Let α_B be associated with the matrix $\bar{\alpha}_B$ with column order different from $j_1, \ldots, j_m$ then $\bar{\alpha}_B = \alpha_B P$, where P is a permutation matrix. As $P^{-1} = P^\tau$, the starting problem can be written in the form:

$$\min \bar{\gamma}_B^\tau \bar{y}_B + \gamma_N^T x_N,$$
$$\bar{\alpha}_B \bar{y}_B + \alpha_N x_N = \beta,$$
$$\bar{y}_B \geq 0, \quad y_N \geq 0,$$

where $\bar{y}_B = P^{-1} y_B$, $\bar{\gamma}_B = P^{-1} \gamma_B$, hence the canonical form is obtained:

$$\min \quad \bar{\gamma}_B^\tau \ (\bar{\alpha}_B)^{-1}\beta + (\gamma_N^\tau - \bar{\gamma}_B^\tau(\bar{\alpha}_B)^{-1}\alpha_N)y_N,$$

$$\text{subj.} \quad \bar{y}_B \ + (\bar{\alpha}_B)^{-1}\alpha_N x_N = (\bar{\alpha}_B)^{-1}\beta, \qquad (2.1.0.3)$$

$$\bar{y}_B \ \geq 0, \quad y_N \geq 0.$$

Since the $\bar{\gamma}_B^\tau(\bar{\alpha}_B)^{-1} = \gamma_B^\tau(P^{-1})^\tau(P^{-1})\alpha_B^{-1} = \gamma_B^T A_B^{-1}$, these are free terms and coefficient vectors in the objective functions problems (2.1.0.1) and (2.1.0.3) are equal, while the system of equations in (2.1.0.3) can be write in the form $P^{-1}(y_B + \alpha_B^{-1}\alpha_N x_N) = P^{-1}\beta$,, i.e., it is about by permuting the equations of the system in (2.1.0.1). $\square$

We will use the linear programming problem in the symmetric form:

Definition 2.1.1. *The problem* (??) *is basically admissible if* $\beta_i \geq 0$ *for every* $i = 1, \ldots, m$

The previous definition is closely related to the notion of a basic permissible solution. Namely, if we introduce additional slack variables, we get:

$$min\omega(y) = \sum_{i=1}^{n} \gamma_i y_i + d \qquad (2.1.0.4)$$

$$\text{p.o} \sum_{j=1}^{n} \alpha_{ij} y_j - \beta_i = -y_{n+i}, i = 1, \ldots, m. \qquad (2.1.0.5)$$

The form (2.1.0.5) is often called the *canonical* form of linear programming problems. The variables on the right (in this case $y_{n+1}, \ldots, y_{n+m}$) are called *basic* while those on the left-hand side of the equations (in this case $y_1, \ldots, y_n$)*non-basic*. We will further label the variables with $y_{B,1}, \ldots, y_{B,m}$ and $y_{N,1}, \ldots, y_{N,n}$, respectively. If we now put $y_{N,1} = \ldots = y_{N,n} = 0$, then $y_{B,i} = \beta_i$ for $i = 1, \ldots, m$. The solution thus obtained is basically admissible, if $\beta_i \geq 0$ for each $i = 1, \ldots, m$.

Corollary 2.1.1. *Let* (2.1.0.5) *in the basic admissible canonical form be* $\gamma_j \geq 0$ *for every* $j = 1, \ldots, n$. *Then the basic solution* $y^* = (0, \ldots, 0, \beta_1, \ldots, \beta_m)$ *is optimal.*

The fundamental feature of the canonical form is that it is based on the coefficients can determine whether the basis is correct sizing optimally, as in which case the target function is unbounded from below:

Theorem 2.1.2. *Let it be in canonical form* (2.1.0.3)

$$\gamma_j' \geq 0, j \in N, \ \beta_i' \geq 0, \ss = 1, \ldots, m.$$

Then the basic solution corresponding to the base α_B *is optimal.*

Proof. From $y_N^* = 0$ it follows $y_B^* = \beta' \geq 0$, so y^* is permissible solution. If y is an arbitrary admissible solution, then from $y \geq 0$ i $y_j^* = 0$, $j \in N$ follows:

$$\gamma^T x = d' + \sum_{j \in N} \gamma_j' y_j \geq d' = d' + \sum_{j \in N} \gamma_j' y_j^* = \gamma^T x^*,$$

so y^* is the optimal solution. $\square$

Theorem 2.1.3. *Let it be in canonical form* (3.1.2) $\beta_i' \geq 0$, $i = 1, \ldots, m$ *and for some* $k \in N$ *is valid that* $\gamma_k' < 0$ *i* $\alpha_{ik}' \leq 0$, $i = 1, \ldots, m$. *Then the target function on the permissible set is unbounded from below:*

Proof. Let $t \geq 0$ be the coordinates of the point $y(t)$ defined by:

$$y_{j_i}(t) = \beta_i' - \alpha_{ik}'t, \; i = 1, \ldots, m, \quad y_j(t) = 0, \; j \in N\backslash\{k\}, \quad y_k(t) = t.$$

It is directly verified that $y(t)$ is the admissible point of the problem (2.1.1) and is valid.

$$\gamma^T x(t) = d' + \sum_{j \in N} \gamma_j' y_j(t) = d' + \gamma_k' t \rightarrow -\infty, \quad t \rightarrow \infty.$$

$\square$

Unless the requirements of Theorems 3.1.2 or 3.1.3 can then be switched to the canonical form that corresponds to some new neighbor base but so that the value of the target function in the new one reduce, or at least not increase, the basic permissible solution. That idea is in the basic simplex method. It is used in this *spreadsheet* linear programming problems.

Elemental Transformations LP-tables are:

1. multipliing i−th row with $\sigma \neq 0$, for $i \in \{1, \ldots, m\}$, 2. adding i−th row, for $i = 1, \ldots, m$, j-–th row for $j \in \{0, 1, \ldots, m\}$.

Lemma 2.1.2. *The LP-table is finally applied a lot of elements transform transforms to LP-table corresponding to equivalent linear programming problem.*

Proof. Elementary transformations with i− of this type for *and* $\in$ $\{1, \ldots, m\}$ obviously do not change the allowed set. Add i− of this type for $i \in \{1, \ldots, m\}$ zero type transforms it into a species.

$$[-d + \beta_i \,|\, \gamma_1 + \alpha_{i1} \cdots \gamma_n + \alpha_{in}],$$

corresponding to the new target function:

$$
\begin{aligned}
\omega &= d - \beta_i + (\gamma_1 + \alpha_{i1})y_1 + \cdots + (\gamma_n + \alpha_{in})y_n \\
&= d + \gamma_1 y_1 + \cdots + \gamma_n x_n + (-\beta_i + \alpha_{i1}y_1 + \cdots + \alpha_{in}y_n) \\
&= d + \gamma_1 y_1 + \cdots + \gamma_n x_n,
\end{aligned}
$$

i.e., on the admissible set of values of the transformed objective function, the starting target functions are the same, so the problems are equivalent. $\square$

It follows from Lemma 3.1.2 that by a procedure analogous to Gauss-Jordan, different formulations of the problem are obtained by the method.

In this chapter, we will present a simplex method for solving problems linear programming. This method was developed in 1940 by George B. Danzig. We will first show an algebraic approach, which is suitable when it is about the task of smaller size, and then we will give the forgiveness simplex algorithm using the so-called simplex table.

2.2   The Algebraic Essence of the Simplex Method

Let the following linear problem be given programming with $r = m$ li ne ar no independent constraints:

$$\min \quad \omega(y) = \gamma^T x = \sum_{i=1}^{n} \gamma_i x_i$$

$$\text{p.o} \quad \sum_{j=1}^{n} \alpha_{ij} y_j = \beta_i, \quad i = 1, \ldots, m,$$

$$y_j \geq 0, \quad j = 1, \ldots, n.$$

The optimal solution lies in one of the convex polyhedron foundations, where at least $k = n - m$ variables equal to zero. Let us choose arbitrarily k variables for the independent (free) variables and by means of expressing them dependent variables. Let the independent variables $y_1, \ldots, y_k$ such that when we use them to express $m = n - k$ dependent variables:

$$-y_{k+1} = \alpha_{k+1,1} y_1 + \alpha_{k+1,2} y_2 + \cdots + \alpha_{k+1,k} y_k - \beta_{k+1}$$

$$\cdots$$

$$-y_n = \alpha_{n,1} y_1 + \alpha_{n,2} y_2 + \cdots + \alpha_{n,k} y_k - \beta_n \quad (2.2.0.1)$$

the coefficients $\beta_{k+1}, \ldots, \beta_n$ are positive. The target function at point $y = (y_1, \ldots, y_k)$ gets a value:

$$\omega(y_1, \ldots, y_n) = \omega(y_1, \ldots, y_k) = \gamma_0 + \gamma_1 y_1 + \cdots + \gamma_k x_k. \quad (2.2.0.2)$$

Assuming $y_1 = y_2 = \cdots = y_k = 0$ we get a basic solution:

$$(\underbrace{0, 0, \ldots, 0}_{k}, \beta_{k+1}, \beta_{k+2}, \ldots, \beta_n), \quad \beta_{k+1}, \ldots, \beta_n \geq 0$$

and minimum value:

$$\omega = \gamma_0.$$

Let us now consider whether we can reduce the value of the objective function ω by increasing it one of the variables $y_1, y_2, \ldots, y_k$. If all the coefficients $\gamma_1, \gamma_2, \ldots, \gamma_k$ with $y_1, y_2, \ldots, y_k$ of the target function is positive, then it magnifies one of these pro's (to values greater than zero) we cannot reduce the value goal functions. This means that the basic solution is obtained and is optimal. However, if between the coefficients $\gamma_1, \gamma_2, \ldots, \gamma_k$ has and negative, then magnifying the value of the variable in front of which the coefficient in the function of the target is negative, we can reduce the value of the function goal ω, i.e., we can come up with a better basic solution. For example, let be a negative coefficient γ_j in the expression (2.2.0.2). Now it makes sense to increase the variable y_j and thus go beyond of the basic solution obtained, where y_j was equal to zero, to a new basic solution where instead of y_j will be zero some of the dependent variables. Increasing y_j decreases the value functions of the ω target, but we need to make sure that some of the dependents are doing this $y_{k+1}, y_{k+2}, \ldots, y_n$ does not become negative. Oh no, obviously they will not become negative if they are in the equations (2.2.0.1) coefficients $\alpha_{k+1,j}, \ldots, \alpha_{nj}$ with y_j negative, so then y_j can be increased indefinitely, for some $j, 1 \leq j \leq k$. This means that the target function is not bounded on the bottom (i.e., $\omega_{\min} = -\infty$). In this case, the problem does not have the optimal solution. Suppose now that between the coefficients of y_j in the equations (2.2.0.1) there are also positive coefficients. For example, let it be in the singular expressing the dependent variable y_i, $i \in \{k+1, \ldots, n\}$

$$-y_i = \alpha_{i1}y_1 + \cdots + \alpha_{ij}y_j + \cdots + \alpha_{ik}y_k - \beta_i$$

positive coefficient with y_j, i.e., $\alpha_{ij} > 0$. If we put it $y_1 = \cdots = y_{j-1} = y_{j+1} = \cdots = y_k = 0$, we get the system:

$$-y_{k+1} = \alpha_{k+1,j}y_j - \beta_{k+1}$$

$$\cdots$$

$$-y_n = \alpha_{n,j}y_j - \beta_n.$$

This means that y_j can be increased to a value:

$$\frac{\beta_i}{\alpha_{ij}}, \quad \beta_i > 0, \alpha_{ij} > 0, \beta = k+1, \ldots, n$$

because for that value of variable y_j the variable y_i becomes zero: $y_i = 0$. Further increasing y_j the variable y_i would become negative. Now let's choose between the variables $y_{k+1}, y_{k+2}, \ldots, y_n$ variable y_p by condition:

$$\frac{\beta_p}{\alpha_{pj}} = \min\left\{ \frac{\beta_i}{\alpha_{ij}}, \quad \alpha_{ij} > 0, k+1 \le i \le n \right\}.$$

Then the value y_j is expressed from the equation:

$$-y_p = \alpha_{p1}y_1 + \cdots + \alpha_{p,j}y_j + \cdots + \alpha_{pk}y_k - \beta_p$$

and substitutes in the other equations (2.2.0.1) and in the function of the objective (2.2.0.2). That way, instead of the variable y_j among the independent variable is a variable y_p, and the pro men li va y_j, which was in the previous the basic solution was independent, now it becomes a dependent variable. Symbolically, we designate this change as $y_p \leftrightarrow y_j$. So the variables are dependent now:

$$y_j, y_{k+1}, \cdots, y_{p-1}, y_{p+1}, \cdots, y_n.$$

These dependent variables are expressed by independent variables:

$$y_1, \cdots, y_{j-1}, y_{j+1}, \cdots, y_k, y_p.$$

Also, the target function is expressed by independent variables.

The performed procedure is now being repeated. If all the coefficients are with independent changes li ve $y_1, \ldots, y_{j-1}, y_{j+1}, \cdots, y_k, y_p$ in the function of the objective positive, then for

$$y_j = y_{k+1} = \cdots = y_{p-1} = y_{p+1} = \cdots = y_n = 0$$

basic solution obtained and optimal solution. If there are also negative coefficients with independent changes, the procedure is repeated until it is added to the optimal solution.

Let, in the general case, be given a basic admissible problem (2.1.0.5) for which $\gamma_j < 0$ for some $j \in \{1, \ldots, n\}$ i $\alpha_{ij} > 0$ for some $i \in \{1, \ldots, m\}$. Given $\gamma_j < 0$, it makes sense to increase the variable $y_{N,j}$ and thus go beyond of the basic solution obtained, where $y_{N,j}$ was equal to zero, to a new basic solution where instead of $y_{N,j}$ will be zero some of the dependent variables. Increasing $y_{N,j}$ decreases the value functions of the $\omega(y)$ target, but we need to make sure that some of the basic ones are $y_{B,1}, y_{B,2}, \ldots, y_{B,m}$ do not become negative. If $\alpha_{sj} < 0$, the variable $y_{B,s}$ will obviously not become negative. Now consider the equation:

$$-y_{B,i} = \alpha_{i1} y_{N,1} + \ldots + \alpha_{ij} y_{N,j} + \ldots + \alpha_{in} y_{N,n} - \beta_i$$

If we put $y_{N,1} = \cdots = y_{N,j-1} = y_{N,j+1} = \cdots = y_{N,n} = 0$, we get:

$$-y_{B,1} = \alpha_{1j} y_{N,j} - \beta_i$$

$$\cdots$$

$$-y_{B,m} = \alpha_{nj} y_{N,j} - \beta_n.$$

This means that $y_{N,j}$ can be increased up to:

$$\frac{\beta_i}{\alpha_{ij}}, \quad \beta_i > 0, \alpha_{ij} > 0,$$

because for this value of the variable $y_{N,j}$ the variable $y_{B,i}$ becomes zero. Further increasing $y_{N,j}$ the variable $y_{B,i}$ would become negative. Let us now choose the basic variable $y_{B,p}$ by condition:

$$\frac{\beta_p}{\alpha_{pj}} = \min\left\{ \frac{\beta_i}{\alpha_{ij}}, \quad \alpha_{ij} > 0, k+1 \leq i \leq n \right\}. \qquad (2.2.0.3)$$

Now we replace the variables $y_{B,p}$ and $y_{N,j}$, i.e., we now express the variable $y_{N,j}$ from equation:

$$-y_{B,p} = \alpha_{p1} y_{N,1} + \cdots + \alpha_{pj} y_{N,j} + \cdots + \alpha_{pn} y_{N,n} - \beta_p$$

and replace it in the other equations and in the function of the goal. That way, instead of the variable $y_{N,j}$ among the non-base variable is a variable $y_{B,p}$, and the pro men li va $y_{N,j}$ which is in the previous the basic solution was independent, now it becomes a dependent variable. This gives us a new basic solution:

$$y^1 = (y_N^1, y_B^1) = \left((0, \ldots, 0, \beta_p^1, 0, \ldots, 0), (\beta_1^1, \ldots, \beta_{p-1}^1, 0, \beta_{p+1}^1, \ldots, \beta_n^1) \right)$$

where:

$$\beta_p^1 = \frac{\beta_p}{\alpha_{pj}}, \quad \beta_l^1 = \beta_l - \alpha_{lj}\frac{\beta_p}{\alpha_{pj}}, \quad l \neq p$$

As well as the equivalent problem in canonical form. At point y^1, the goal function has a larger value than in the basic, basic admissible solution. If we now continue to apply the same procedure with the new one in canonical form, the goal function will increase, and at some point, we will surely get into the situation that we can apply a lemma (??) or come to the conclusion that the objective function unlimited. This intuitive consideration is crucial to the simplex method, and will be more formally implemented in the next section. Also, we will introduce the notion of Tucker's table, which in many respects simplifies the procedure just described for constructing a new basic solution. This is the most common approach to benefit when implementing simplex methods.

2.3 The Term Tucker's Tables and the Simplex Method for Basic Permissible Canonical Forms

Consider one canonical form of linear programming problem:

$\max f(y) = \gamma_1 y_{N,1} + \ldots + \gamma_n y_{N,n} + d$

$\text{subj.} \alpha_{11} y_{N,1} + \alpha_{12} y_{N,2} + \ldots + \alpha_{1n} y_{N,n} - \beta_1 = -y_{B,1}$

$\qquad \alpha_{21} y_{N,1} + \alpha_{22} y_{N,2} + \ldots + \alpha_{2n} y_{N,n} - \beta_2 = -y_{B,2}$ (2.3.0.1)

$\qquad \ldots\ldots\ldots$

$\qquad \alpha_{m1} y_{N,1} + \alpha_{m2} y_{N,2} + \ldots + \alpha_{mn} y_{N,n} - \beta_m = -y_{B,m}.$

The problem can be summarized in the following way:

$y_{N,1}$	$y_{N,2}$	$\cdots$	$y_{N,n}$	-1		
α_{11}	α_{12}	$\cdots$	α_{1n}	β_1	$=$	$-y_{B,1}$
α_{21}	α_{22}	$\cdots$	α_{2n}	β_2	$=$	$-y_{B,2}$
$\vdots$	$\vdots$	$\ddots$	$\vdots$	$\vdots$		$\vdots$
α_{m1}	α_{m2}	$\cdots$	α_{mn}	β_m	$=$	$-y_{B,m}$
γ_1	γ_2	$\cdots$	γ_n	d	$=$	f

(2.3.0.2)

We call this table **Tucker Table** for the problem (2.3.0.1). Let us introduce the labels $\alpha_{m+1,j} = \gamma_j$ for $j = 1, \ldots, n$ as well as $\alpha_{i,n+1} = \beta_i$ for $i = 1, \ldots, n$. Also, let $\alpha_{m+1,n+1} = d$. Now, to describe the canonical form is linear programming sufficient*expanded Tucker's table*: $\overline{A} = \{\alpha_{ij}\}_{i=\overline{1,m+1}, j=\overline{1,n+1}}$. Below, we will often identify matrices $\overline{A}$ and A whenever there is no risk of confusion.

Two forms of Tucker tables are encountered in the literature, where $y_1, \ldots, y_n$ are non-base, and $t_1, \ldots, t_m$ are base variables.

At the end of the previous section, it was necessary to express non-base variable $y_{N,j}$ from the p equation of the system (2.3.0.1) and replace it in other equations and as a function of the goal. In this way, the variable $y_{B,p}$ becomes non-basic, while $y_{N,j}$ becomes basic.

Now let's look at what happens to the A' matrix of the appropriate standard form (2.1.0.2). In the matrix A' the columns corresponding to the basic variables form a unit matrix while the others form Tucker's A table. After replacing the column variables $K_{v_{N,j}}$ of the matrix A' becomes equal to p that column unit matrices. To do this, it suffices to subtract for each $i = 1, \ldots, m$, and $\neq p$ of the and type matrix A' p-that type multiplied by:

$$\frac{a^{\iota}_{i,v_{n,j}}}{a'_{p,v_{n,j}}} = \frac{\alpha_{ij}}{\alpha_{pj}}, \quad A^{\iota} = [a'_{ij}]_{i=\overline{1,m},\, j=\overline{1,m+n}}$$

while we only divide p by $\alpha_{pj} = a^{\iota}_{p,v_{n,j}}$. In the same way, we transform the vector β^{ι} and the objective function by counting them in the order $n + m + 1$ column and the $m + 1$ type of matrix A'. We describe this transformation in vector and scalar form as follows:

$$V^1_q = V_q - \frac{\alpha_{qj}}{\alpha_{pj}} V_p, \quad (a')^1_{ql} = a'_{ql} - \frac{a'_{pl} a'_{q,v_{B,j}}}{a'_{p,v_{B,j}}} \tag{2.3.0.3}$$

Where V_i is note for i-th row $A'_{i\bullet}$ of matrix A'. In this case, new Tucker table is equal to:

$$A^1 = \begin{array}{cccccccc} y_{N,1} & \cdots & y_{N,j-1} & y_{B,p} & y_{N,j+1} & \cdots & y_{N,n} & -1 \\ a^1_{11} & \cdots & a^1_{1,j-1} & a^1_{1j} & a^1_{1,j+1} & \cdots & a^1_{1n} & \beta^1_1 =-y_{B,1} \\ a^1_{21} & \cdots & a^1_{2,j-1} & a^1_{2j} & a^1_{2,j+1} & \cdots & a^1_{2n} & \beta^1_2 =-y_{B,2} \\ \vdots & & \vdots & \vdots & \vdots & & \vdots & \vdots \end{array}$$

$$\tag{2.3.0.4}$$

$$
\begin{array}{ccccccc}
a^1_{p-1,1} & \cdots & a^1_{p-1,j-1} & a^1_{p-1,j} & a^1_{p-1,j+1} & \cdots & a^1_{p-1,n} & \beta^1_{p-1}=-y_{B,p-1} \\
a^1_{p1} & \cdots & a^1_{p,j-1} & a^1_{pj} & a^1_{p,j+1} & \cdots & a^1_{pn} & \beta^1_p = -y_{B,j} \\
a^1_{p+1,1} & \cdots & a^1_{p+1,j-1} & a^1_{p+1,j} & a^1_{p+1,j+1} & \cdots & a^1_{p+1,n} & \beta^1_{p+1}=-y_{B,p+1} \\
\vdots & & \vdots & \vdots & \vdots & & \vdots & \vdots & \vdots \\
a^1_{m1} & \cdots & a^1_{m,j-1} & a^1_{mj} & a^1_{m,j+1} & \cdots & a^1_{mn} & \beta^1_m = -y_{B,m} \\
\gamma^1_1 & \cdots & \gamma^1_{j-1} & \gamma^1_j & \gamma^1_{j+1} & \cdots & \gamma^1_n & d^1 = f
\end{array}
$$

where the elements a^1_{ql} are given by the expression:

$$
\begin{aligned}
\alpha^1_{pj} &= \frac{1}{\alpha_{pj}}; \\
\alpha^1_{pl} &= \frac{\alpha_{pl}}{\alpha_{pj}}, & l \neq j; \\
\alpha^1_{qj} &= -\frac{\alpha_{qj}}{\alpha_{pj}}, & q \neq p; \\
\alpha^1_{ql} &= \alpha_{ql} - \frac{\alpha_{pl}\alpha_{qj}}{\alpha_{pj}}, & q \neq p, \neq j;
\end{aligned}
\tag{2.3.0.5}
$$

Of course, we mean here that $q = 1, \ldots, m+1$ and $l = 1, \ldots n+1$. Expressions (2.3.0.5) are derived directly from expressions (2.3.0.3) if the structure of the matrix A' is considered.

2.4 Algorithm of Simplex Method

We consider linear program:

$$\max \omega(y) = \omega(y_{N,1}, \ldots, y_{N,n_1}) = \sum_{i=1}^{n_1} \gamma_i y_{N,i} - d$$

$$N_i^{(1)} : \quad \sum_{j=1}^{n_1} \alpha_{ij} y_{N,j} \leq \beta_i, \quad i = 1, \ldots, r$$

$$N_i^{(2)} : \quad \sum_{j=1}^{n_1} \alpha_{ij} y_{N,j} \geq \beta_i, \quad i = r+1, \ldots, s \quad (2.4.0.1)$$

$$J_i : \quad \sum_{j=1}^{n_1} \alpha_{ij} y_{N,j} = \beta_i, \quad i = s+1, \ldots, m$$

$$y_{N,j} \geq 0, \quad j = 1, \ldots, n_1.$$

In this case, α_{ij}, β_i and γ_j are known real numbers. Any inequality of the form $N_i^{(1)}$ (*LE* constraints) is transforms into the appropriate equation by adding *slack* variables $y_{B,i}$:

$$N_i^{(1)} : \quad \sum_{j=1}^{n_1} \alpha_{ij} y_{N,j} + y_{B,i} = \beta_i, \quad i = 1, \ldots, r.$$

Also, any inequality of the form $N_i^{(2)}$ (*GE* constraint) is transforms into equality by subtracting *surplus* (*offset*) variables $y_{B,i}$:

$$N_i^{(2)} : \quad \sum_{j=1}^{n_1} \alpha_{ij} y_{N,j} - y_{B,i} = \beta_i, \quad i = r+1, \ldots, s.$$

That way, we get a linear program in standard form:

$$\max \quad \gamma_1 y_1 + \cdots + \gamma_{n_1} y_{n_1} - d$$

$$\text{subj.} \quad Ay = \beta,$$

$$\beta = (\beta_1, \ldots, \beta_m), \quad y = (y_{N,1}, \ldots, y_{N,n_1}, y_{B,1}, \ldots, y_{B,m})$$

$$y_{N,j} \geq 0, j = 1, \ldots, n_1, \qquad\qquad (2.4.0.2)$$

$$y_{B,i} \geq 0, \text{ß} = 1, \ldots, s, \quad y_{B,i} = 0, \text{ß} = s + 1, \ldots, m$$

where the matrix A belongs to the set $\mathbb{R}^{m \times (n_1+s)}$.

In each equation, we choose one of the variables $y_{N,j}$ for which apply $\alpha_{p,j} <> 0$ to the base one, and make the corresponding substitutions in other equations. An algorithm can be used to replace the base one variables $y_{B,p} = 0$ and nonbasic $y_{N,j}$. After replacing $n = n_1 + s$, the canonical form of the problem (2.4.0.2) can be written in the following table form τ_0: Beginning table τ_0

height	$y_{N,1}$	$y_{N,2}$	$\cdots$	$y_{N,n}$	-1	
	α_{11}^0	α_{12}^0	$\cdots$	α_{1n}^0	β_1^0	$= -y_{B,1}$
	$\cdots$	$\cdots$	$\cdots$	$\cdots$	$\cdots$	$\cdots$
	α_{m1}^0	α_{m2}^0	$\cdots$	α_{mn}^0	β_m^0	$= -y_{B,m}$
	γ_1^0	γ_2^0	$\cdots$	γ_n^0	d^0	$= \omega^0$

where $y_{N,1}, \ldots, y_{N,n}$ non-basic variables i $y_{B,1}, \ldots, y_{B,m}$ base variables. Table (2.4) transforms the coefficients of the matrix A and the vector γ denoted by α_{ij}^0 and γ_j^0, respectively. Table (2.4) is called Tucker's corresponding to maximize the goal function.

Definition 2.4.1. *The solution of a linear code programming task whose independent variables are equal to zero is called the basic solution.*

Proposition 2.4.1. *Let Tucker be a table of basic maximization the task of li ne ar nog programming represented by a table of* τ_k *forms:*

Table τ_k *in the* k *iteration.*

height$y_{N,1}$	$y_{N,2}$	$\cdots$	$y_{N,n}$	*-1*	
α_{11}^k	α_{12}^k	$\cdots$	α_{1n}^k	β_1^k	$= -y_{B,1}$
$\cdots$	$\cdots$	$\cdots$	$\cdots$	$\cdots$	$\cdots$
α_{m1}^k	α_{m2}^k	$\cdots$	α_{mn}^k	β_m^k	$= -y_{B,m}$
γ_1^k	γ_2^k	$\cdots$	γ_n^k	d^k	$= \omega^k$

If $\beta_1^k, \ldots, \beta_m^k \geq 0$, *then in the base-admissible maximization, the basic solution in the table is an acceptable solution.*

Proof. Indeed, putting all the independent variables equal Zero, all major ogs are reduced to equations $-\beta_i^k = -y_{B,i}$ or $\beta_i^k = y_{B,i}$. In this way, every solution satisfies all limitations task, so it is admissible. $\square$

The following is a simplex algorithm for maximizing the base admissible table τ_k (2.4.1).

Algorithm SimplexStandardMax

(A simplex method for maximizing the base admissible table).

k-th an iteration of the simplex method consists of the following steps: *Step 1.* If $\gamma_1^k, \ldots, \gamma_n^k \leq 0$, the algorithm stalls. Basic the admissible solution corresponding to the simplex table τ_k is optimal. *Step 2.* Select arbitrary $\gamma_j^k > 0$. (Can be taken maximum $\gamma_j^k > 0$. Selecting the first $\gamma_j^k > 0$ solves the cycling problem.)

Step 3. For every l for which $\gamma_l^k > 0$, examine whether $\alpha_{il}^k \geq 0$ for each $i = 1, \ldots, m$. If such l there is a barn algorithm. Target the function on the admissible set is unbounded from above, i.e., the maximum is $+\infty$.

This step is a modification of the corresponding step from [43]. Modification consists in being a condition from Step 3 checks for every l for which $\gamma_l^k > 0$ applies, not just $l = j$.

Step 4. Calculate

$$\min_{1 \le i \le m} \left\{ \frac{\beta_i^k}{\alpha_{ij}^k}, \quad \alpha_{ij}^k > 0 \right\} = \frac{\beta_p^k}{\alpha_{pj}^k}$$

and replace the non-base variable $y_{N,j}$ and the base variable $y_{B,p}$. Symbolically, this transformation is written as follows mode: $y_{N,j} \leftrightarrow y_{B,p}$.

This transformation is described in more detail in the **Replace** algorithm.

Algorithm Replace.

(Substitution of the base variable $y_{B,p}$ and the non-base variable $y_{N,j}$.)

Lead element transformation:

$$\alpha_{pj}^{k+1} = \frac{1}{\alpha_{pj}^k}. \tag{2.4.0.3}$$

Transformation of an element into a leading species, excluding the leading element:

$$\alpha_{pl}^{k+1} = \frac{\alpha_{pl}^k}{\alpha_{pj}^k}, \quad l \ne j, \tag{2.4.0.4}$$

Transform a vector element β into a leading type:

$$\beta_p^{k+1} = \frac{\beta_p^k}{\alpha_{pj}^k}, \tag{2.4.0.5}$$

Transformation of an element in the leading circle, except for the leading element:

$$\alpha_{qj}^{k+1} = -\frac{\alpha_{qj}^{k}}{\alpha_{pj}^{k}}, \quad q \neq p, \tag{2.4.0.6}$$

Transformation of an element beyond the leading type and the leading column:

$$\alpha_{ql}^{k+1} = \alpha_{ql}^{k} - \frac{\alpha_{pl}^{k}\alpha_{qj}^{k}}{\alpha_{pj}^{k}}, \quad q \neq p, l \neq j; \tag{2.4.0.7}$$

Transform a vector element β outside the leading type:

$$\beta_{q}^{k+1} = \beta_{q}^{k} - \frac{\beta_{p}^{k}\alpha_{qj}^{k}}{\alpha_{pj}^{k}}, \quad q \neq p \tag{2.4.0.8}$$

Transform the vector element γ into a leading type:

$$\gamma_{j}^{k+1} = -\frac{\gamma_{j}^{k}}{\alpha_{pj}^{k}}, \tag{2.4.0.9}$$

Transform a vector element γ outside the leading type:

$$\gamma_{l}^{k+1} = \gamma_{l}^{k} - \frac{\gamma_{j}^{k}a_{pl}^{k}}{\alpha_{pj}^{k}}, \quad l \neq j; \tag{2.4.0.10}$$

Free member transformation d:

$$d^{k+1} = d^{k} - \frac{\beta_{p}^{k}\gamma_{j}^{k}}{\alpha_{pj}^{k}}. \tag{2.4.0.11}$$

Step 5. Replace k with $k+1$ and go to Step 1.

Consider the *Replace algorithm.*

The equation expressing the basic variable $y_{B,p}$ is of the form:

$$\sum_{l=1}^{n} \alpha_{pl}^{k} y_{N,l} - \beta_{p}^{k} = -y_{B,p}$$

hence obtained after replacement:

$$\sum_{l=1,l\neq j}^{n} \frac{\alpha_{pl}^{k}}{\alpha_{pj}^{k}} y_{N,l} + \frac{1}{\alpha_{pj}^{k}} y_{B,p} - \frac{\beta_{p}^{k}}{\alpha_{pj}^{k}} = -y_{N,j}. \qquad (2.4.0.12)$$

Equations are derived from there (2.4.0.3)–(2.4.0.5). For $q \neq p$ from

$$\sum_{l=1}^{n} \alpha_{ql}^{k} y_{N,l} - \beta_{q}^{k} = -y_{B,q}$$

$$\sum_{l=1,l\neq j}^{n} \alpha_{ql}^{k} y_{N,l} - \alpha_{qj}^{k} \left(\sum_{l=1,l\neq j}^{n} \frac{\alpha_{pl}^{k}}{\alpha_{pj}^{k}} y_{N,l} + \frac{1}{\alpha_{pj}^{k}} y_{B,p} - \frac{\beta_{p}^{k}}{\alpha_{pj}^{k}} \right) - \beta_{p}^{k} = -y_{B,q},$$

i.e.:

$$\left(\alpha_{q1}^{k} - \frac{\alpha_{p1}^{k} \alpha_{qj}^{k}}{\alpha_{pj}^{k}} \right) y_{N,1} + \cdots + \left(\alpha_{q,j-1}^{k} - \frac{\alpha_{p,j-1}^{k} \alpha_{qj}^{k}}{\alpha_{pj}^{k}} \right) y_{N,j-1}$$

$$- \frac{\alpha_{qj}^{k}}{\alpha_{pj}^{k}} y_{B,p}$$

$$+ \left(\alpha_{q,j+1}^{k} - \frac{\alpha_{p,j+1}^{k} \alpha_{qj}^{k}}{\alpha_{pj}^{k}} \right) y_{N,j+1} + \left(\alpha_{qn}^{k} - \frac{\alpha_{pn}^{k} \alpha_{qj}^{k}}{\alpha_{pj}^{k}} \right) y_{N,n}$$

$$- \left(\beta_{q}^{k} - \frac{\beta_{p}^{k} \alpha_{qj}^{k}}{\alpha_{pj}^{k}} \right) = -y_{B,q}.$$

That's where they come from (2.4.0.6)–(2.4.0.8). Finally, from:

$$\omega^k = \gamma_1^k y_{N,1} + \cdots + \gamma_n^k y_{N,n} - d^k$$

and (2.4.0.12) we get:

$$\omega^k = \sum_{l=1,l\neq j}^{n} \gamma_l^k y_{N,l} - \gamma_j^k \left(\sum_{l=1,l\neq j} \frac{\alpha_{pl}^k}{\alpha_{pj}^k} y_{N,l} + \frac{1}{\alpha_{pj}^k} y_{B,p} - \frac{\beta_p^k}{\alpha_{pj}^k} \right) - d^k,$$

i.e.:

$$
\begin{aligned}
\omega^k =\ & \left(\gamma_1^k - \frac{\gamma_j^k \alpha_{p1}^k}{\alpha_{pj}^k} \right) y_{N,1} + \cdots + \left(\gamma_{j-1}^k - \frac{\gamma_j^k \alpha_{p,j-1}^k}{\alpha_{pj}^k} \right) y_{N,j-1} \\
& - \frac{\gamma_j^k}{\alpha_{pj}^k} y_{B,p} \\
& + \left(\gamma_{j+1}^k - \frac{\gamma_j^k \alpha_{p,j+1}^k}{\alpha_{pj}^k} \right) y_{N,j+1} + \left(\gamma_n^k - \frac{\gamma_j^k \alpha_{pn}^k}{\alpha_{pj}^k} \right) y_{N,n} \\
& - \left(d^k - \frac{\beta_p^k \gamma_j^k}{\alpha_{pj}^k} \right).
\end{aligned}
$$

That's where they come from (2.4.0.9), (2.4.0.10) i (2.4.0.11).

This transformation is similar to the Gaussian elimination process:

- select $p = \alpha_{ij} \neq 0$;

- exchange $y_{N,j}$ i $y_{B,i}$;

- change p sa $1/p$;

- change each value q in ith row with q/p;

- change each value r in column j sa $-r/p$;

- change another value s sa $s - (q \cdot r/p)$.

Remark 2.4.1. *In the general case, the indices p and j in Step 3 are not unambiguous from re where ni, i.e., there may be more candidates who meet the above requirements. When p and j are selected, they determine the so-called pivot element α_{pj} with which they are performed transformations in Step 4. Transition from table τ_k to table τ_{k+1} is called pivoting. A series of elementary transformations in Step 4 it makes one complex, the so-called transformation. The following theorem proves that pivoting does not increases the target function and that τ_{k+1} is also a simplex table.*

Simplex algorithm method for minimizing base admissible table (2.4.1) is similar to the maximization table algorithm: **Algorithm SimplexStandardMin**

(Simplex method for minimizing the base admissible table, as in [55, 64]).

k-th iteration of the simplex method consists of the following steps:

Step 1. If $\gamma_1^k, \ldots, \gamma_n^k \geq 0$, the algorithm stops. The base admissible solution corresponding to the simplex table τ_k is optimal.

Step 2. Select arbitrary $\gamma_j^k < 0$. (Minimum $\gamma_j^k < 0$ or first may be taken $\gamma_j^k < 0$.)

Step 3. Examine whether $\alpha_{ij}^k \leq 0$ for each $i = 1, \ldots, m$. If this condition is satisfied, the algorithm stops. Target the function on the admissible set is unbounded from below, i.e., the minimum is $-\infty$.

Step 4. Calculate

$$\min_{1\leq i\leq m}\left\{\frac{\beta_i^k}{\alpha_{ij}^k},\quad \alpha_{ij}^k>0\right\}=\frac{\beta_p^k}{\alpha_{pj}^k}$$

and replace the non-base variable $y_{N,j}$ and the base variable $y_{B,p}$, using the *Replace* algorithm.

Step 5. Change k with $k+1$ and go to step 1.

This practically means that the table τ_k applies the following elemental transformations:

- multiply p−th row with $-\frac{\alpha_{qj}^k}{\alpha_{pj}^k}$ and add to rows $q=0,\dots,m$, $q\neq p$;
- divide p-th row with α_{pj}^k.

Theorem 2.4.1. *By applying the elemental transformations described in Step 4. The algorithm SimplexStandardMin is obtained from the simplex table τ_k simplex table τ_{k+1} corresponding to an equivalent linear problem programming. Here $d^{k+1}\geq d^k$.*

Proof. Based on Lemma 2.1.2, the table τ_{k+1} corresponds to the equivalent linear programming problem. In doing so, it exits the basic matrix a column that had a unit in $p-$ that type and a $j-$ that column enters. Based on previous considerations about moving to an adjacent base, out of condition:

$$\frac{\beta_p^k}{\alpha_{pj}^k}=\min\left\{\frac{\beta_i^k}{\alpha_{ij}^k}\,|\,\alpha_{ij}^k>0\right\}$$

follows y^{k+1} basic permissible solution, i.e., $\beta_i^{k+1}\geq 0$. The proof follows from:

$$\beta_i^{k+1}=\beta_i^k-\frac{\beta_p^k\alpha_{ij}^k}{\alpha_{pj}^k}$$

i.e.,

$$\frac{\beta_p^k}{\alpha_{pj}^k} \leq \frac{\beta_i^k}{\alpha_{ij}^k}.$$

From $\gamma_j^k < 0$ follows:

$$-d^{k+1} = -d^k + \frac{\gamma_j^k}{\alpha_{pj}^k}\beta_p^k \leq -d^k,$$

i.e., $d^{k+1} \geq d^k$. □

Let's now apply the *SimplexStandardMin* algorithm to the example already discussed in 2.1.0.2:

Example 2.4.1. To problem

$$5y_1 - 4y_2,$$

$$y_1 + y_2 \leq 80,$$

$$3y_1 + y_2 \leq 180,$$

$$y_1 + 3y_2 \leq 180,$$

$$y_1 \geq 0, y_2 \geq 0$$

fits simplex table τ_0 : (pivot elements are framed for transparency), $\tau_0 =$

y_1	y_2	-1	
1	1	80	$= -y_3$
$\boxed{3}$	1	180	$= -y_4$
1	3	180	$= -y_5$
-5	-4	0	$= \omega$

The corresponding basic permissible solution is $y^0 = (0, 0, 80, 180, 180)$, *and the value of the objective function* $\gamma^\tau y^0 = 0$. *Obviously, the tests in steps 1 and 2 are not satisfied. Let us choose* $j = 1$. *Now*

$$\beta_1^0/\alpha_{11}^0 = 80, \ \beta_2^0/\alpha_{21}^0 = 60, \ \beta_3^0/\alpha_{31}^0 = 180,$$

from where we determine $p = 2$. So, we need a replacement $y_1 \leftrightarrow y_4$. The Replace algorithm is obtained following a series of transformations as well as the corresponding table τ_1:

$$\alpha_{21}^1 = \alpha_{pj}^1 = \frac{1}{\alpha_{pj}^0} = 1,$$

$$\alpha_{22}^1 = \alpha_{pl}^1 = \frac{\alpha_{pl}^0}{\alpha_{pj}^0} = \frac{\alpha_{22}^0}{\alpha_{21}^0} = \frac{1}{3},$$

$$\alpha_{11}^1 = \alpha_{qj}^1 = -\frac{\alpha_{qj}^0}{\alpha_{pj}^0} = -\frac{\alpha_{11}^0}{\alpha_{21}^0} = -\frac{1}{3},$$

$$\alpha_{31}^1 = \alpha_{qj}^1 = -\frac{\alpha_{qj}^0}{\alpha_{pj}^0} = -\frac{\alpha_{31}^0}{\alpha_{21}^0} = -\frac{1}{3}\alpha_{31}^0 - \frac{\alpha_{21}^0 \alpha_{31}^0}{\alpha_{21}^0} = 1 - \frac{3 \cdot 1}{3} = \frac{2}{3},$$

$$\alpha_{12}^1 = \alpha_{ql}^1 = \alpha_{ql}^0 - \frac{\alpha_{pl}^0 \alpha_{qj}^0}{\alpha_{pj}^0} = \alpha_{12}^0 - \frac{\alpha_{22}^0 \alpha_{11}^0}{\alpha_{21}^0} = 1 - \frac{1 \cdot 1}{3} = \frac{2}{3},$$

$$\alpha_{32}^1 = \alpha_{ql}^1 = \alpha_{ql}^0 - \frac{\alpha_{pl}^0 \alpha_{qj}^0}{\alpha_{pj}^0} = \alpha_{32}^0 - \frac{\alpha_{22}^0 \alpha_{31}^0}{\alpha_{21}^0} = 3 - \frac{1 \cdot 1}{3} = \frac{8}{3}.$$

$$\beta_1^1 = \beta_q^1 = \beta_q^0 - \frac{\beta_p^0 \alpha_{qj}^0}{\alpha_{pj}^0} = \beta_1^0 - \frac{\beta_2^0 \alpha_{11}^0}{\alpha_{21}^0} = 80 - \frac{80 \cdot 1}{3} = 20,$$

$$\beta_2^1 = \beta_p^1 = \frac{\beta_p^0}{\alpha_{pj}^0} = \frac{\beta_2^0}{\alpha_{21}^0} = \frac{180}{3} = 60,$$

$$\beta_3^1 = \beta_q^1 = \beta_q^0 - \frac{\beta_p^0 \alpha_{qj}^0}{\alpha_{pj}^0} = \beta_3^0 - \frac{\beta_2^0 \alpha_{31}^0}{\alpha_{21}^0} = 180 - \frac{180 \cdot 1}{3} = 120.$$

$$\gamma_1^1 = \gamma_j^1 = -\frac{\gamma_j^0}{\alpha_{pj}^0} = -\frac{\gamma_1^0}{\alpha_{21}^0} = -\frac{-5}{3} = \frac{5}{3},$$

$$\gamma_2^1 = \gamma_l^1 = \gamma_l^0 - \frac{\gamma_j^0 \alpha_{pl}^0}{\alpha_{pj}^0} = \gamma_2^0 - \frac{\gamma_1^0 \alpha_{22}^0}{\alpha_{21}^0} = -4 - \frac{-5 \cdot 1}{3} = -\frac{7}{3},$$

$$d^1 = d^0 - \frac{\beta_2^0 \gamma_1^0}{\alpha_{21}^0} = 0 - \frac{180 \cdot (-5)}{3} = -300.$$

y_4	y_2	-1	
$-\frac{1}{3}$	$\frac{2}{3}$	*20*	$= -y_3$
$\frac{1}{3}$	$\frac{1}{3}$	*60*	$= -y_1$
$-\frac{1}{3}$	$\frac{8}{3}$	*120*	$= -y_5$
$\frac{5}{3}$	$-\frac{7}{3}$	*300*	$= \omega$

$\tau_1 =$

Now the solution $y^1 = (60, 0, 20, 0, 120)$, which correspond to value of goal function $\gamma^T x^1 = -300$. Tests in steps 1 and 2 are not allowed. Now $j = 2$ and

$$\beta_1^1/\alpha_{12}^1 = 30, \beta_2^1/\alpha_{22}^1 = 180, \beta_3^1/\alpha_{32}^1 = 45,$$

and it is valid $p = 1$. The following change should be made $y_2 \leftrightarrow y_3$. From Algorithm*Replace* we have the next transformations and the corresponding table τ_2:

$$\alpha_{12}^2 = \alpha_{pj}^2 = 1,$$

$$\alpha_{11}^2 = \alpha_{pl}^2 = \frac{\alpha_{pl}^1}{\alpha_{pj}^1} = \frac{\alpha_{11}^1}{\alpha_{12}^1} = -\frac{1}{2},$$

$$\alpha_{22}^2 = \alpha_{qj}^2 = -\frac{\alpha_{qj}^1}{\alpha_{pj}^1} = -\frac{\alpha_{22}^1}{\alpha_{12}^1} = -\frac{1}{2},$$

$$\alpha_{32}^2 = \alpha_{qj}^2 = -\frac{\alpha_{qj}^1}{\alpha_{pj}^1} = -\frac{\alpha_{32}^1}{\alpha_{12}^1} = -4,$$

$$\alpha_{21}^2 = \alpha_{ql}^2 = \alpha_{ql}^1 - \frac{\alpha_{pl}^1 \alpha_{qj}^1}{\alpha_{pj}^1} = \alpha_{21}^1 - \frac{\alpha_{11}^1 \alpha_{22}^1}{\alpha_{12}^1} = \frac{7}{6},$$

$$\alpha_{31}^2 = \alpha_{ql}^2 = \alpha_{ql}^1 - \frac{\alpha_{pl}^1 \alpha_{qj}^1}{\alpha_{pj}^1} = \alpha_{31}^1 - \frac{\alpha_{11}^1 \alpha_{32}^1}{\alpha_{12}^1} = 1.$$

$$\beta_1^2 = \beta_p^2 = \frac{\beta_p^1}{\alpha_{pj}^1} = \frac{\beta_1^1}{\alpha_{12}^1} = \frac{20}{2/3} = 30,$$

$$\beta_2^2 = \beta_q^2 = \beta_q^1 - \frac{\beta_p^1 \alpha_{qj}^1}{\alpha_{pj}^1} = \beta_2^1 - \frac{\beta_1^1 \alpha_{22}^1}{\alpha_{12}^1} = 60 - \frac{20 \cdot 1/3}{2/3} = 50,$$

$$\beta_3^2 = \beta_q^2 = \beta_q^1 - \frac{\beta_p^1 \alpha_{qj}^1}{\alpha_{pj}^1} = \beta_3^1 - \frac{\beta_1^1 \alpha_{32}^1}{\alpha_{12}^1} = 120 - \frac{20 \cdot 8/3}{2/3} = 40.$$

$$\gamma_2^2 = \gamma_j^2 = -\frac{\gamma_j^1}{\alpha_{pj}^1} = -\frac{\gamma_2^1}{\alpha_{11}^1} = \frac{7}{2},$$

$$\gamma_1^2 = \gamma_l^2 = \gamma_l^1 - \frac{\gamma_j^1 \alpha_{pl}^1}{\alpha_{pj}^1} = \gamma_1^1 - \frac{\gamma_2^1 \alpha_{11}^1}{\alpha_{12}^1} = \frac{5}{3} - \frac{-7/3 \cdot (-1/3)}{2/3} = \frac{1}{2},$$

$$d^2 = d^1 - \frac{\beta_1^1 \gamma_2^1}{\alpha_{12}^1} = 300 - \frac{20 \cdot (-7/3)}{2/3} = 370.$$

$\tau_2 =$

y_4	y_3	-1	
$-\frac{1}{2}$	$\frac{3}{2}$	30	$= -y_2$
$\frac{1}{2}$	$-\frac{1}{2}$	50	$= -y_1$
1	-4	40	$= -y_5$
$\frac{1}{2}$	$\frac{7}{2}$	370	$= \omega$

The base admissible solution is $y^2 = (50, 30, 0, 0, 40)$, and the objective function takes the value $\gamma^T x^2 = -370$. As the test in Step 1 is satisfied, this is a y^2 optimal solution, a the value of the objective function is $\omega = -370$.

Note that each simplex table corresponds to one extreme point together Γ_P, so that the simplex method represents a "walk" in the dark. Since $d^{k+1} < d^k$, that no peak can be to repeat. Since the number of vertices is finite, it follows that there are finitely many iterations that come either to the optimal solution or to the conclusion that the target function is not restricted from below.

Remark 2.4.2. *More than one value of p can occur for which the fragment $\frac{\beta_p^k}{\alpha_{pj}^k}$ is the smallest. Then arbitrarily, p can be selected. In the following chapters, we will say more about this.*

Theorem 2.4.2. *If $\gamma_1^k, \ldots, \gamma_n^k \leq 0$ the target function has the extremum at the point $y_{N,i} = 0$, $i = 1, \ldots, n$.*

Proof. Suppose $y_{N,1}, \ldots, y_{N,n}$ arbitrary nonnegative numbers. Then it works:

$$\omega(y) = \sum_{i=1}^{n} \gamma_i^k y_{N,i} - d^k \leq -d^k$$

because $\gamma_i^k y_{N,i} \leq 0$ for each $i = 1, \ldots, n$. Equality applies if and only if $y_{N,i} = 0$, $i = 1, \ldots, N$. $\square$

Theorem 2.4.3. *Make it for someone* $j \in \{1, \ldots, n\}$ $\gamma_j^k > 0$ *i* $\alpha_{ij}^k \leq 0$ *for each* $i = 1, \ldots, m$, *then the objective function is unlimited.*

Proof. If $\alpha_{ij}^k \leq 0$ for each $i = 1, \ldots, m$, considering restrictions

$$\alpha_{i1}^k x_{N,1} + \cdots + \alpha_{ij}^k x_{N,j} + \cdots + \alpha_{in}^k x_{N,N} - \beta_i^k = -y_{B,i}, \text{ß} = 1, \ldots, m,$$

the variable $y_{N,j}$ can be increased indefinitely without any the dependent variable $y_{B,and}$ is not negative. Since $\gamma_j^k > 0$, so with increasing the variable y_j also increases the value of the target function. This means that the target function is unlimited. $\square$

In the general case, $\gamma_j^k > 0$ for some j and $\alpha_{ij}^k > 0$ for some i. We will show that the table (2.4.1) can be transformed into an equivalent, with one independent and dependent variable swapping places. Let's choose p so that:

$$\frac{\beta_p^k}{\alpha_{pj}^k} = \min_{1 \leq i \leq m} \left\{ \frac{\beta_i^k}{\alpha_{ij}^k} | \alpha_{ij}^k > 0 \right\}. \tag{2.4.0.13}$$

We can replace the variable $y_{N,j}$ from the equation:

$$y_{B,p} = \beta_p^k - (\alpha_{p1}^k x_{N,1} + \cdots + \alpha_{pj}^k x_{N,j} + \cdots + \alpha_{pn}^k x_{N,n})$$

and replace it in all other equations and in the function of the goal. In this way we get a system equivalent to the system (2.4.0.2) now $y_{B,p}$ independent a $y_{N,j}$ dependent variable. They still are the free terms β_i in all equations are positive as γ_j^k becomes not positive. The proof of this assertion (the following theorem) as well as the algorithm for the transformation of the system of equations (2.4.0.2) (to replace the variables $y_{B,p}$ and $y_{N,j}$) will be shown below. We now apply the same procedure as long as one of the numbers γ_j is positive. When all γ_j^k is positive, an admissible solution is obtained $y_{N,1} = \cdots = y_{N,n} = 0$ is optimal, i.e., the objective function reaches the extremum.

Theorem 2.4.4. *If $\beta_1^k, \ldots, \beta_m^k \geq 0$ and if index p selected according to the criterion (3.3.15) and $\gamma_j^k > 0$, then and after the change of place $y_{B,p}$ and $y_{N,j}$ variables $\beta_1^{k+1}, \ldots, \beta_n^{k+1} \geq 0$. It is also i $\gamma_j^{k+1} < 0$.*

Proof. According to the variable replacement algorithm $y_{B,p}$ i $y_{N,j}$ after the transformation is:

$$\beta_q^{k+1} = \frac{\alpha_{pj}^k b_q^k - \alpha_{qj}^k b_p^k}{\alpha_{pj}^k}.$$

If $\alpha_{qj}^k \geq 0$, considering $\frac{\beta_p^k}{\alpha_{pj}^k} \leq \frac{\beta_q^k}{\alpha_{qj}^k}$ we get:

$$\beta_q^{k+1} = \frac{\alpha_{pj}^k b_q^k - \alpha_{qj}^k \beta_p^k}{\alpha_{pj}^k} \geq \frac{\alpha_{pj}^k b_q^k - \alpha_{pj}^k b_q^k}{\alpha_{pj}^k} = 0.$$

Now suppose it is $\alpha_{qj}^k < 0$. Considering $-\frac{\alpha_{qj}^k b_p^k}{\alpha_{pj}^k} > 0$, we get:

$$\beta_q^{k+1} = \frac{\alpha_{pj}^k b_q^k - \alpha_{qj}^k b_p^k}{\alpha_{pj}^k} > \beta_q^k > 0.$$

After the shift, we get it:

$$\gamma_j^{k+1} = -\frac{\gamma_j^k}{\alpha_{pj}^k} < 0,$$

by which the theorem is proved. $\square$

Element α_{pj} we will call the pivot element a the replacement of the variables $y_{B,p}$ and $y_{N,j}$ we will call it replacement by the key element α_{pj}^k.

Example 2.4.2. Solve the following linear problem:

$$\begin{aligned}
\max \quad & \Lambda = 7y_1 + 5y_2 \\
\text{subj.} \quad & 2y_1 + 3y_2 + y_3 = 19 \\
& 2y_1 + y_2 + y_4 = 13 \\
& 3y_2 + y_5 = 15 \\
& 3y_1 + y_6 = 18.
\end{aligned}$$

Solution. The rank of the system matrix and the expanded matrix is 4. This means that we can take 4 variables for bases (for example y_3, y_4, y_5, y_6), and two variables (y_1, y_2) for independent (free).

$$y_3 = 19 - 2y_1 - 3y_2$$
$$y_4 = 13 - 2y_1 - y_2$$
$$y_5 = 15 - 3y_2$$
$$y_6 = 18 - 3y_1$$

In addition, we conclude on the basis of the objective function:

$$\Lambda - 7y_1 - 5y_2 = 0.$$

The latter are negative coefficients −7 and −5. Take the smallest negative coefficient, −7. Then in the column for y_1 we notice three positive elements: 2,2,3. Let's share these numbers are correspondingly free members. The minimum of these ratios is:

$$\min\left\{\frac{19}{2}, \frac{13}{2}, \frac{18}{3}\right\} = \frac{18}{3}.$$

The intersection of type for y_6 and columns for y_1 is number 3. So, the variables y_1 and y_6 swap roles. The new base is y_3, y_4, y_5, y_1, while the independent variables are y_2, y_6. In order to get 1 at the intersection point, we divide the observed species by 3. The rest we add to the species a split type, previously multiplied by the number such that u the column corresponding to y_2, below and above the leading element, we get zeros.

The same procedure is continued in the new table. The last one is negative coefficient −5. In the column for y_2 we notice two positive elements: 3,1,3. We divide by these numbers the corresponding free members. The minimum of these ratios is:

$$\min\left\{\frac{7}{3}, \frac{1}{1}, \frac{15}{3}\right\} = \frac{1}{1}.$$

In the intersection of type for y_4 and columns for y_2 is number 1. Now the variables y_2 and y_4 swap roles. They make a new base y_3, y_2, y_5, y_1, while the independent variables are y_4, y_6. To the other species, we add another species, previously multiplied by the number such that u column y_2 below and above the leading element, we get zeros.

The procedure is repeated in the last table.

$$\min\left\{\frac{4}{4/3}, \frac{12}{2}, \frac{6}{1/3}\right\} = \frac{4}{4/3}$$

Now the variables y_6 and y_3 are swapping roles. They make a new base y_6, y_2, y_5, y_1, while the independent variables are y_3, y_4.

The new species for Λ has no negative coefficients. The maximum target value of function is $\Lambda_{max} = 50$, and is obtained for base $\{5, 3, 0, 0, 6, 3\}$.

Remark 2.4.3. *If there are more than one equals in an iteration of the minimum quantities β_i/α_{ip}, it is necessary to choose the type for which is the ratio of the elements of the next column to those of the column that we use the smallest to solve. This process is repeated until we arrive to the single-digit minimum element β_j/α_{jp}.*

The simplex model of a linear programming type of maximum type is a system of non-equilibrium forms:

$$\alpha_{11}y_1 + \alpha_{12}y_2 + \cdots + \alpha_{1m}y_m \leq \beta_1$$
$$\alpha_{21}y_2 + \alpha_{22}y_2 + \cdots + \alpha_{2m}y_m \leq \beta_2$$
$$\cdots$$
$$\alpha_{n1}y_1 + \alpha_{n2}y_2 + \cdots + \alpha_{nm}y_m \leq \beta_n$$

We translate this system of inequalities into a system of equations, by introducing additional pro's, as follows:

$$\alpha_{11}y_1 + \alpha_{12}y_2 + \cdots + \alpha_{1m}y_m + y_{m+1} = \beta_1$$
$$\alpha_{21}y_2 + \alpha_{22}y_2 + \cdots + \alpha_{2m}y_m + y_{m+2} = \beta_2$$
$$\cdots$$
$$\alpha_{n1}y_1 + \alpha_{n2}y_2 + \cdots + \alpha_{nm}y_m + y_{m+n} = \beta_n$$

The criteria function takes the form:

$$G(y) = \sum_{j=1}^{n} c_j x_j + 0 \cdot (\gamma_{n+1} y_{n+1} + \cdots + \gamma_{n+m} y_{n+m}) \, .$$

Based on this model, we set a zero simplex table of forms:

max ST - 0

where: C – coefficient vector γ_i with the variables y_i of the criterion function, $i = 1, \ldots, n$; γ_β – vector of coefficients as a function of the criteria with variables that make up the basic admissible solution. At max ST - 0, the value of these coefficients is 0; y_β – vector of variables of the basic admissible solution; B – the vector of the values of the variables of the base allowable solution for the observed ite ra ci ju; y_j – base vector multipliers; $G_j - \gamma_j$ – optimality criterion. Based on this criterion, it is decided whether a solution was obtained maximum. The solution is maximum if the condition is fulfilled.

$$(\forall j) G_j - \gamma_j \geq 0.$$

In case the solution is not optimal, this criterion determines the vector that enters the base, which is a vector y_j that satisfies the condition:

$$\min_j \left\{ G_j - \gamma_j | G_j - \gamma_j < 0 \right\}.$$

On the other hand, on the basis of the "theta" criterion, it is determined which vector exits the base, i.e.:

$$\theta = \min_i \left\{ \frac{\beta_i}{\alpha_{ij}}, \quad \alpha_{ij}^k > 0 \right\} = \frac{\beta_p}{\alpha_{pj}}.$$

Procedure for Finding the Optimal Solution by Simplex Method

The general problem of linear programming is considered. Need to find the negative values of the variables $y_1, \ldots, y_k$ that will fill a restriction system given by linear inequalities and equations 1.5.0. 1, and provide the maximum value of the criterion function:

$$\omega_0 = \sum_{j=1}^{k} \gamma_j y_j.$$

We solve the linear programming problem, thus formulated the simplex method according to the following procedure:

1) We translate all inequalities of systems into equations. If it is an unequal of type "$\leq$," then we add the corresponding one variable; if the inequality is of type "$\geq$" then we subtract the corresponding offset variable from the left foreign inequalities. With leveling variables in the function, the criteria are always zero.

News variables are added to all equations and unequal "type" $\geq$. With these variables in function criteria, we put the coefficients M.

2) From the coefficients of the custom model, we compile the initial simplex table. The vector space for the initial solution is made up of unit vectors. These are the vectors that correspond to the "added" variable (add the equalization and all expert).

3) We calculate coefficients for an additional row of simplex tables $G_j - \gamma_j$ for every j. The simplex table contains the initial solution.

4) Let's check the order coefficients $(G_j - \gamma_j)$:

If $G_j - \gamma_j \geq 0$ for every j, then we claim that the optimal solution is found.

If there is $G_j - \gamma_j < 0$, then we choose:

$$G_s - \gamma_s = \left[\min_j (G_j - \gamma_j)\right] < 0.$$

The coefficient $(G_s - \gamma_s)$ corresponds to the vector α_s, so we determine that the vector α_s enters the new vector base.

5) Vector coordinates B we divide by the corresponding positive coordinates of the vector α_s and determine

$$\theta = \frac{\beta_r}{\alpha_{rs}} = \min_i \frac{\beta_i}{\alpha_{is}} \quad (\alpha_{is} > 0).$$

The smallest value of these ratios corresponds to vector α_r, so we determine that the vector α_r should come out of the initial base.

6) We calculate the coefficients for the new simplex table at the coefficients from the initial simplex table according to the transformation rules described.

7) We return to point 4) of this procedure. Each the next iteration begins with step 4) and repeats the procedure until 7) until all the differences are found in 4) $G_j - \gamma_j \geq 0$. Then the process ends, the optimal solution to the linear problem is found.

Example 2.4.3. Solve the system of inequalities by applying the simplex method if the following criteria and constraints are given:

$$\begin{aligned}
\max \quad & G(y) = 10y_1 + 12y_2 + 10y_3 \\
\text{subj.} \quad & 4y_1 + 5y_2 + 4y_3 \leq 4200 \\
& 2y_1 = 2y_2 + y_3 \leq 1500 \\
& 2y_1 + 3y_2 + 4y_3 \leq 2400
\end{aligned}$$

Based on this model, we will form a starting simplex table, max ST-0.

$$\max \quad G(y) = 10y_1 + 12y_2 + 10y_3$$
$$\text{subj.} \quad 4y_1 + 5y_2 + 4y_3 + y_4 = 4200$$
$$2y_1 + 2y_2 + y_3 + y_5 = 1500$$
$$2y_1 + 3y_2 + 4y_3 + y_6 = 2400$$

This table contains the optimal solution, which is:

$$y^* = [0, 720, 60, 360, 0, 0]^\tau, \quad G(y^*) = G_{\max} = 9240.$$

2.5 Determination of the Initial Basic Permissible Solution

The implementation of the *SimplexStandardMax* algorithm implies that one is known basic permissible solution. This is fulfilled if they are all restrictions of type $\leq$ and if $\beta_i \geq 0$, $i = 1, \ldots, m$, or if all constraints of type $\geq$ and if $\beta_i \geq is$, $i = 1, \ldots, m$. By adding leveling variables, we immediately form the base permissible solution. However, in the general case, the underlying permissible solution is unknown. We prove the theorem on a basis for determining the basic admissible solution if the set of permissible solutions to the linear programming problem is blank.

The algorithm has been described so far (the *SimplexStandard-Max/Simp leks Ba sic Min* algorithm) to find the optimal solution, if any, when in the basic form tasks it looks for the maximum/minimum of the objective function and when they are initial maximization/minimization tables are basically permissible. What to do if the basic linear programming task table starts not basic permissible? Before we can apply the simplex method, the algorithm must first be transformed into a maximization table with a basic allowable solution. That's how it is described; the algorithm must first introduce the steps of such a transformation. Consider a simplex algorithm finally for the maximization table in the general case.

Definition 2.5.1. *The basic task of linear programming with maximization is unacceptable if there is no acceptable solution.*

Theorem 2.5.1. *If* $\alpha_{i1}^k, \ldots, \alpha_{in}^k \geq 0$ *i* $\beta_i^k < 0$ *then the and equations in the system* (2.3.2) *have no solution, i.e., the system is intolerable.*

Proof. With the above assumptions, we get:

$$-y_{B,i} = \alpha_{i1}^k x_{N,1} + \cdots \alpha_{in}^k x_{B,N} - \beta_i^k \geq -\beta_i^k > 0,$$

that is, $y_{B,and} < 0$, which contradicts the starting point assuming that all variables are nonnegative. $\square$

In this section, we will discuss the problem of finding the first basic permissible solution (canonical form). Most commonly, two types of methods are used to solve this problem. One group of methods is called the *two-phase simplex method*, and the second type is the *BigM methods* (BigM methods). Three approaches are described here. The two approaches are the so-called phase simplex method. One method requires the introduction of artificial variables and thus increases the dimensions of the problem, while the other does not require the use of artificial variables. The third method combines these two stages into one, and is called the *BigM* method.

2.6 Two-Phase Simplex Methods

The two-phase simplex method consists of two phases, phase I and phase II. Phase I is trying to find someone initial basic feasible solution. When the initial basic permissible solution is found, then Phase II is applied to find the optimal solution. A simplex method is an iterative procedure whose each iteration is characterized by the determination of m basis variables $y_{B,1}, \ldots, y_{B,m}$ and n non-base variables $y_{N,1}, \ldots, y_{N,n}$.

Geometrically, the simplex method moves from one extreme point (angle) to the set of admissible solutions in the second, while improving the values of the objective function in each iteration. The two-phase simplex method goes through two phases, phase I and phase II. Phase I attempts an extremely extreme point from above. Once the initial extreme point is found once, phase II is applied to resolve the original LP.

Example 2.6.1. For

$$-y_1 - y_2$$
$$2y_1 + 3y_2 \leq 24, 2y_1 - y_2 \leq 8, y_1 - 2y_2 \leq 2,$$
$$-y_1 + 2y_2 \leq 8, y_1 + 3y_2 \geq 6, 3y_1 - y_2 \geq 3,$$
$$0 \leq y_1 \leq 7, 0 \leq y_2 \leq 7$$

Phase I of the simplex algorithm ends at the extreme point indicated by (a) in the following figure. Then Phase II follows a sequence of extreme points marked by arrows along the edges of a set of admissible solutions. The optimum extreme point is indicated by (d).

If $\beta \geq 0$ and if all nonbasic variables $y_{N,1}, \ldots, y_{N,n}$ are equal to zero, then $y_{B,1} = \beta_1, \ldots, y_{B,m} = \beta_m$ base admissible solution. If the condition $\beta \geq 0$ is not met, it is necessary to find an initial basic admissible solution or to determine that it does not exist. There are several strategies for Phase I.

2.6.1   A Two-Phase Simplex Method That Uses Artificial Variables

The classic approach is to associate a linear program in standard form the so-called *widespread problem* [3, 13].

Let the linear programming problem be given in standard form:

$$\gamma^T x,$$
$$\text{subj.} \quad Ay = \beta, \qquad\qquad (2.6.1.1)$$
$$y \geq 0.$$

J it is only fair that we can assume that u the standard form $\beta \geq 0$ (otherwise we multiply the corresponding equations by -1). We attach to the problem (2.6.1.1) an auxiliary linear programming problem:

$$\min \quad e^T w,$$
$$\text{subj.} \quad Ay + w = \beta, \qquad\qquad (2.6.1.2)$$
$$y \geq 0, \ w \geq 0,$$

where $e = (1, \ldots, 1) \in \mathbb{R}^m$ and $w \in \mathbb{R}^m$ is a vector of so-called. *artificial* variables. The important fact is that the set of admissible solutions to the problem (2.6.1.2) is empty because its gur no belongs to it point ($y = 0$, $w = \beta$). It is also clear that the target function is on that set bottom bounded by zero. The permissible base consists of columns that correspond to the variables $w_1, \ldots, w_m$, a the canonical form of the problem (2.6.1.2) is obtained by eliminating w from the objective function using Eq $w = \beta - Ay$. Problems (2.6.1.1) and (2.6.1.2) are related by the following theorem:

Theorem 2.6.1. *The set of admissible solutions to the problem (2.6.1.1) is non-empty if and only if the optimal value of the objective function problems (2.6.1.2) equal to zero.*

Proof. Let $\bar{y}$ be a valid solution (2.6.1.1). Then $(\bar{y}, 0)$ is an admissible solution to the problem (2.6.1.2), with the value of the objective function is zero. Since zero is the lower bound for the objective function of the problem (2.6.1.2), it follows that $(\bar{y}, 0)$ is optimal solution and that zero is the optimal value of the objective function of the problem. Suppose now that $(\bar{y}, \bar{w})$ is the optimal solution to the problem (2.6.1.2) and suppose $e^\tau \bar{w} = 0$. From $e > 0$, $\bar{w} \geq 0$ follows $\bar{w} = 0$, so we have $A\bar{y} = \beta$, i.e., $\bar{y}$ is a permissible solution to the problem (2.6.1.2). □

The previous theorem is based on the so-called *two-phase modification of simplex methods.*

Algorithm 2. (Two-phase modification of simplex methods). *I Faza:*

II Faza:

Step 1. All are removed from the last simplex table non-basic columns corresponding to artificial variables, the null type is replaced by the type $[0|\ \gamma_1 \ \ldots \ \gamma_n \ 0 \ \ldots \ 0]$ which has a $n + k + 1$ element, with

k being the number of basic news öf variables. The resulting LP table is reduced to a simplex table by eliminating those $\gamma_j \neq 0$ that correspond to the base variables.

Step 2. If $k = 0$ go to Step 3. If $k > 0$ there are basic columns in the simplex table that correspond to artificial ones variable. Note the basic column corresponding to the artificial one variable w_s. Let that column contain a unit of type v. Two cases are possible:

1. All elements of type v except the base unit are zero. Then is the type v and the column corresponding to the variable w_s omitted from the simplex table. 2. In addition to the basic unit, let $r-$ be an element of type v different from zero. Obviously, $r > 0$ because it is in the zero column an artificial variable w_s that equals zero, and that $r-$ ta the column does not match the artificial variable because they are missing all columns corresponding to non-basic variables. Stozernom by transforming with the pivotal element α_{vs}, make $r-$ tu column basic and then omit the column corresponding to the variable w_s because this is now a non-base column corresponding to an artificial variable. Replace k with $k - 1$ and repeat Step 2.

Step 3. The resulting simplex table contains columns only that correspond to the changes in the problem (2.6.1.1). Apply Algorithm 1.

Note that Algorithm 2 obviously ends in a finite number of steps.

An example to illustrate Algorithm 2 is taken from [13].

Example 2.6.2. Determine the solution to the following problem:

$$\min \quad y_1 - y_2 + y_3,$$
$$\text{subj.} \quad y_1 + y_2 + 2y_3 + y_4 = 3,$$
$$-y_2 - y_3 + y_4 = 3,$$
$$y_1 - y_2 + 3y_4 = 9,$$
$$y \geq 0.$$

As the basic admissible solution is not known, we will apply a two-phase modification of the simplex algorithm. *I Phase.*

An associated problem is:

$$\min \quad w_1 + w_2 + w_3,$$

	y_1	$+y_2$	$+2y_3$	$+y_4$	$+w_1$			=	3,
subj.		$-y_2$	$-y_3$	$+y_4$		$+w_2$		=	3,
	y_1	$-y_2$		$+3y_4$			$+w_3$	=	9,

$$y \geq 0, \quad w \geq 0,$$

and is matched by the following LP table:

0	0	0	0	0	1	1	1
3	1	1	2	1	1	0	0
3	0	-1	-1	1	0	1	0
9	1	-1	0	3	0	0	1

hence by eliminating units from zero species (by subtracting all other types of zero) gets a simplex table (below are pivot elements framed):

-15	-2	1	-1	-5	0	0	0
3	[1]	1	2	1	1	0	0
3	0	-1	-1	1	0	1	0
9	1	-1	0	3	0	0	1

Using a simplex algorithm we get a new simplex table:

−9	0	3	3	−3	−2	0	0
3	1	1	2	1	1	0	0
3	0	−1	−1	1	0	1	0
6	0	−2	−2	$\boxed{2}$	−1	0	1

As there are negative elements in the zero column, again we apply a simplex algorithm:

0	0	0	0	0	1/2	0	3/2
0	1	2	3	0	2	0	−1/2
0	0	0	0	0	−1/2	1	−1/2
3	0	−1	−1	1	−1/2	0	1/2

As the optimal value of the auxiliary problem $\min e^T w = 0$, we move on to the second stage.

Phase II. By removing the non-base columns that correspond artificial variables (fifth and seventh) and coefficient replacement zero-type LP table is given by the corresponding coefficients of the starting problem:

0	1	−1	1	0	0
0	1	2	3	0	0
0	0	0	0	0	1
3	0	−1	−1	1	0

where, after eliminating the unit in the zero row of the first column, gets a simplex table:

0	0	−3	−2	0	0
0	1	$\boxed{2}$	3	0	0
0	0	0	0	0	1
3	0	−1	−1	1	0

Now we eliminate the second type because it contains all the elements (except coefficient corresponding to an artificial variable) equal to zero and we eliminate the fifth column because all elements are zero. We get a simplex table from which all artificials are eliminated variables:

$$
\begin{array}{ccccc}
0 & 0 & -3 & -2 & 0 \\
0 & 1 & \boxed{2} & 3 & 0 \\
3 & 0 & -1 & -1 & 1
\end{array}
$$

Now all the requirements for Algorithm 1 are fulfilled. The next step is to obtain the optimal solution:

$$
\begin{array}{ccccc}
0 & 3/2 & 0 & 5/2 & 0 \\
0 & 1/2 & 1 & 3/2 & 0 \\
3 & 1/2 & 0 & 1/2 & 1
\end{array}
$$

Another variant of the two-phase simplex method is described in [40] and [55]. This algorithm has the advantage in relation to the extended problem because it does not use artificial variables.

2.6.2 Two-Phase Simplex Method Without Artificial Variables

We will now present one version of the algorithm for determining the initial one a basic admissible solution that does not require the introduction of artificial variables. The main disadvantage of the previous method is the increase in the dimension of the linear problem. We consider the standard form of linear programming problem without restrictions on the sign of the coefficients β_i in which the base is an unknown permissible solution. The existence of a permissible solution follows from the following lemma:

Lemma 2.6.1. *Let $\beta_i = \alpha_{i0}$ be a coefficient for some and. If $\alpha_{ij} \geq 0$, $j = 1, \ldots, n$, then the set of admissible solutions is empty.*

Proof. Given the conditions in the lemma, in the set of restriction, there is an equation in which the sum of the products is negative colors a negative number, which is impossible. □

Let the set of solutions be linear programming is permissible and let y be a basic impermissible solution with q negative coordinates. Let (new numbering if necessary) achieved $y = (y_1, \ldots, y_m, 0, \ldots, 0)$ basic inadmissible solution such that $y_1, \ldots, y_q < 0$, $q \leq m$, and $y_p \geq 0$ for $p > q$. The corresponding base is $K_1, \ldots, K_m$.

If $q = m$, is selected for the element $\alpha_{ms} < 0$ (such exists by Lemma (2.6.1) and by applying a simplex transformation we immediately get a new solution in which at least one coordinate is positive. If $q < m$, we consider $\alpha_{rs} < 0$ for $r = 1, \ldots, q$ (exist by Lemma(2.6.1). If exists $r \in \{1, \ldots, q\}$ i $s \in \{1, \ldots, n\}$ such that:

$$\min_{h>q} \left\{ \frac{y_h}{\alpha_{hs}} \mid \alpha_{hs} > 0 \right\} \geq \frac{y_r}{\alpha_{rs}}, \qquad (2.6.2.\ 1)$$

we choose α_{rs} for the element. Then it is:

$$y^1 = \sum_{j \neq r} \left(y_j - \frac{y_r}{\alpha_{rs}} \alpha_{js} \right) K_j + \frac{y_r}{\alpha_{rs}} K_s.$$

For $j > q$ i $\alpha_{js} < 0$ it is valid $y_j - \dfrac{y_r}{\alpha_{rs}} \alpha_{js} \geq 0$. For $\alpha_{js} \geq 0$ and $j > q$ is:

$$\frac{y_j}{\alpha_{js}} \geq \frac{y_r}{\alpha_{rs}} \alpha_{js} \Leftrightarrow y_j - \frac{y_r}{\alpha_{rs}} \alpha_{js} \geq 0$$

and since $\dfrac{y_r}{\alpha_{rs}} > 0$, it is obvious that y^1 has at most $q - 1$ negative coordinates.

If there is no r such that the condition (2.6.2. 1) is satisfied, let them be now $r \notin \{1, \ldots, q\}$ and $s \in \{1, \ldots, n\}$ such that:

$$\min_{h > q} \left\{ \frac{y_h}{\alpha_{hs}} \,\middle|\, \alpha_{hs} > 0 \right\} = \frac{y_r}{\alpha_{rs}}. \qquad (2.6.2.\ 2)$$

For such r and s, we set α_{rs} for the pivot element. Using a simplex transformation, we get a new solution y^1 in which we prove analogous to the former that the coordinates $y^1_{q+1}, \ldots, y^1_m$ remain nonnegative. As the set of basic solutions is finite, (applying anti-cycling rules if necessary), after many transformations the condition (2.6.2. 1) will be fulfilled. Based on these considerations, the following algorithm is finite. **Algorithm 3.**

(Solving linear programming problems without introducing artificial variables).

Step 1. We form an initial LP form table:

$-d$	γ_1	$\cdots$	γ_n
β_1	α_{11}	$\cdots$	α_{1n}
$\vdots$	$\vdots$		$\vdots$
β_m	α_{m1}	$\cdots$	α_{mn}

If $\beta_i \geq is0$, $i = 1, \ldots, m$, then we apply Algorithm 1.

Step 2. Let $\beta_{i_1}, \ldots, \beta_{i_q} < 0$. If $\alpha_{ij} \geq 0$ for some $i \in \{i_1, \ldots, i_q\}$ i each $j = 1, \ldots, n$, algorithm stops because the set of constraints is unacceptable. Otherwise, we continue.

Step 3. If $q = m$ we choose $\alpha_{ms} < 0$ for the element.

If $q < m$ and if there are $r \in \{i_1, \ldots, i_q\} = I$ and s such that condition fulfilled.

$$\min_{h \notin I} \left\{ \frac{\beta_h}{\alpha_{hs}} \mid \alpha_{hs} > 0 \right\} \geq \frac{\beta_r}{\alpha_{rs}}, \quad \alpha_{rs} < 0,$$

we choose α_{rs} for the element.

If there is no r such that the previous condition is satisfied, let is now r such that:

$$\min_{h \notin I} \left\{ \frac{\beta_h}{\alpha_{hs}} \mid \alpha_{hs} > 0 \right\} = \frac{\beta_r}{\alpha_{rs}}.$$

For such r and s we set α_{rs} for the parent element. *Step 4.* Apply transform and go to Step 1.

Example 2.6.3. Let it be the initial LP chart

720	7	0	0	5	0
−100	−2	0	1	−1	0
−360	−8	0	0	−3	1
180	3	1	0	1	0

Since there are negative coefficients in the zero column, we apply Algorithm 3. The condition (2.6.2. 1) is satisfied in the first column (the pivot elements are framed), and by applying the simplex transformation, we obtain:

405	0	0	0	11/8	7/8
−10	0	0	1	−1/4	−1/4
45	1	0	0	3/8	−1/8
45	0	1	0	−1/8	3/8

In the next step, we again apply Algorithm 3, because $\alpha_{01} < 0$, i we immediately get the optimal solution:

370	0	0	3/2	1/2	0
40	0	0	−4	1	1
50	1	0	−1/2	1/2	0
30	0	1	3/2	−1/2	0

We have proved that if $\Gamma_P \neq \emptyset$ is then basic permissible solution. The condition for the existence of an optimal basic admissible solution is the following lemma.

Lemma 2.6.2. *If the admissible set of problems* (1.5.0.4) *is empty and if the target function on it is bounded from below, then the problem* (1.5.0.4) *has a basic admissible optimal solution.*

Proof. How the target function of the problem (1.5.0. 4) is limited from below, the application of the simplex algorithm to the initial base admissible the solution ends after a lot of steps and that basic permissible optimal solutions. □

A direct consequence of Lemma 2.6.2 is that the existence of an optimal solution withdraws the existence of a basic permissible optimal solution.

The SimplMax/SimplMin algorithm.

Simplex method algorithm forms maximization/minimization tables, which are not basically permissible. The current table is in the form (2.3.4)

Step 1. If $\beta_1^k, \beta_2^k, \ldots, \beta_m^k \geq 0$, we move on to Step 5.

Otherwise, we continue.

Step 2. We choose $\beta_i^k < 0$ (For example, the last one). *Step 3.* If

$\alpha_{i1}^k, \alpha_{i2}^k, \ldots, \alpha_{in}^k \geq 0$, STOP: the maximization task is unacceptable. (We will discuss this case in more detail later).

Otherwise, we continue.

Step 4. If $i = m$, we choose $\alpha_{mj}^k < 0$, we take the key element α_{mj}^k and we go to Step 1. If $i < m$, we choose $\alpha_{ij}^k < 0$ and we calculate:

$$\min_{l > i} \left(\left\{ \frac{\beta_i^k}{\alpha_{ij}^k} \right\} \cup \left\{ \frac{\beta_l^k}{\alpha_{lj}^k}; \alpha_{lj}^k > 0 \right\} \right) = \frac{\beta_p^k}{\alpha_{pj}^k}$$

so we choose α_{pj}^k as the key element (which corresponds to the substitution of the base element variables $y_{B,p}$ and non-base variables $y_{N,j}$). Go to Step 1.

Step 5. Apply a simplex algorithm for base admissible maximization (mini mi za ci onu) table (algorithm *SimplexStandardMax/SimplexStandardMin*).

Remark 2.6.1. *As in algorithm SimplexStandardMax can be more than one value for p for which $\frac{\beta_p^k}{\alpha_{pj}^k}$ is at least. P can be arbitrarily selected.*

Implementation of a simplex algorithm that does not use artificial variables by means of functionalities in MATHEMATICA is described in the [49] monograph.

Example 2.6.4. This example illustrates a general simplex algorithm (the *SimplexMax* algorithm) on a maximization table

y_1	y_2	-1	
-1	-2	-3	$= -t_1$
1	1	3	$= -t_2$
1	1	2	$= -t_3$
-2	4	0	$= \omega$

Solution:

(1) The initial table is obviously a maximization table.

(2) We move on to step (2) because $\beta_1 = -3$ is negative.

(3) We choose $\beta_1 = -3$.

(4) We proceed to step (4), since both coefficients $\alpha_{11} = -1$ and $\alpha_{12} = -2$ are negative.

(5) We can choose $\alpha_{11} = -1$ or $\alpha_{12} = -2$. For the sake of determination we choose $\alpha_{11} = -1$. How $1 = and < m = 3$ is calculated

$$\min\left(\left\{\frac{\beta_1}{\alpha_{11}} = \frac{-3}{-1}\right\} \cup \left\{\frac{\beta_2}{\alpha_{21}} = \frac{3}{1}, \frac{\beta_3}{\alpha_{31}} = \frac{2}{1}\right\}\right) = \frac{\beta_3}{\alpha_{31}}$$

We take the key element α_{31}:

y_1	y_2	-1	
-1	-2	-3	$= -t_1$
1*	1	3	$= -t_2$
1	1	2	$= -t_3$
-2	4	0	$= \omega$

$\Rightarrow$

t_3	y_2	*-1*	
-1	*-1*	*-1*	$= -t_1$
-1	*0*	*1*	$= -t_2$
1	*1*	*2*	$= -y_1$
2	*6*	*4*	$= \omega$

We proceed to step (1).

(1) Apparently!

(2) We move on to step (2) because $\beta_2 = -1$ is negative.

(3) We have to choose $\beta_2 = -1$.

(4) We proceed to step (4), because $\alpha_{12} = -1$ is negative.

(5) We have to choose $\alpha_{12} = -1$. As $1 = and < m = 3$, we calculate

$$\min\left(\left\{\frac{\beta_1}{\alpha_{12}} = \frac{-1}{-1}\right\} \cup \left\{\frac{\beta_3}{\alpha_{32}} = \frac{2}{1}\right\}\right) = \frac{\beta_1}{\alpha_{12}}$$

The key is α_{12}:

t_3	y_2	-1	
-1	-1	-1	$= -t_1$
-1	0	1	$= -t_2$
1	1	2	$= -y_1$
2	6	4	$= \omega$

$\Rightarrow$

t_3	t_1	-1	
-1	-1	1	$= -y_2$
-1	0	1	$= -t_2$
2	1	1	$= -y_1$
8	6	-2	$= \omega$

We proceed to step (1).

(1) *Apparently!*

(2) $\beta_1, \beta_2, \beta_3 \geq 0$, *that is, the table is maximally permissible. We proceed to step (5).*

(5) *Apply a simplex algorithm for maximization tables with basic permissible solutions (let's leave the reader alone complete the task).*

2.7   BigM Method

By combining Phase I and Phase II, an algorithm is obtained that can be solved; there is a very linear programming problem. Finally, note that the essence of the idea of a two-phase modification of the simplex method is as follows: limitations of the starting problem (2.5.1) by introducing artificial ones of the variables $w_1, \ldots, w_m$ to the base admissible solutions while observing the extended objective function.

$$\omega^w = \gamma^T x + M w_1 + \cdots + M w_m,$$

where M is an arbitrarily large coefficient. As long as the artificial variables occur in a basic admissible solution, the optimal solution was not found due to the pro is validity of the coefficient M. So the goal is to use simplex methods to make all artificial variables are eliminated from the basis of the admissible solution and thus equated with zero. When a basic admissible, non-artificial solution is formed variables, we no longer need them because they are in a reduced problem the, requirements for the implementation of Algorithm 1 are fulfilled. The meaning of introducing artificial variables is only to channel the order of performing elementary transformations.

In one embodiment of this method, [13], an auxiliary problem is formed at as follows:

$$\begin{aligned}
\min \quad & \gamma^T x + M e^T w, \\
\text{subj.} \quad & Ay + w = \beta, \\
& y \geq 0, \ w \geq 0,
\end{aligned} \tag{2.7.0.1}$$

where M is a sufficiently large constant. The initial basic solution to this problem is $(0, \beta)$. If, applying the simplex method gives the optimal solution for which some of the variables w_i is a basic starting problem is inadmissible (due to the arbitrariness of the constant M). Otherwise, the solution obtained is optimal for the starting problem. Due to the constant M, this method is often referred to as the **BigM** method. The main disadvantage of this method is the increase in the dimension of the problem and the uncertainty about the choice of the constant M.

Example 2.7.1. Now let's consider a problem that requires a minimum value criteria functions using ***BigM*** methods:

$$\min \quad 160y_1 + 100y_2 + 120y_3,$$
$$\text{subj.} \quad 2y_1 + y_2 + 2y_3 \geq 350,$$
$$y_1 + y_2 + \ y_3 \geq 300, \qquad (2.7.0.2)$$
$$4y_1 + y_2 + 2y_3 \geq 400,$$
$$y_1 \geq 0 \ y_2 \geq 0 \ \& y_3 \geq 0.$$

By introducing equalization variables, we will (2.7.0.2) express in the form of equations. Since the left side is inequality of this system larger than the right, we subtract the leveling variables and we get the following system of equations:

$$2y_1 + y_2 + 2y_3 - y_4 \qquad \qquad = 350$$
$$y_1 + y_2 + \ y_3 \qquad - y_5 \qquad = 300 \qquad (2.7.0.3)$$
$$4y_1 + y_2 + 2y_3 \qquad \qquad - y_6 = 400.$$

The coefficients with the smoothing variables are negative. It means that we cannot determine the initial nonnegative solution in the first simplex table. Therefore, we introduce new variables into the model, the so-called artificial variables. These variables do not belong to the system restrictions and have no specific economic significance, except that serve as a calculating tool. In the process of problem-solving are eliminated from the solution so that they are not in the optimal solution; no artificial variable can occur. If a non-nonnegative problem solution contains at least one positive artificial variable (which cannot be released), then there is no possible solution to the problem.

So that artificial variables do not appear in the optimum solution, we introduce coefficients in the function of criteria with these variables marked with M, where M is a relatively large positive number. [1] So, after expanding the problem with artificial variables, we got the following model:

$$(\min); \omega_0 = 160y_1 + 100y_2 + 120y_3 + 0y_4 + 0y_5 + +0y_6 + Mx_7 + Mx_8 + Mx_9$$

$$
\begin{aligned}
2y_1 + y_2 + 2y_3 - y_4 \qquad\quad + y_7 \qquad\qquad &= 350 \\
y_1 + y_2 + \; y_3 \qquad\quad - y_5 \qquad\quad + y_8 \qquad &= 300 \\
4y_1 + y_2 + 2y_3 \qquad\qquad\;\; - y_6 \qquad\qquad + y_9 &= 400
\end{aligned}
$$

in which all variables must be nonnegative, the initial simplex table can be filled in, and the initial basic solution can be determined. It will be made up of artificial variables.

			160	100	120	0	0	0	M	M	M
C	B	y_0	y_1	y_2	y_3	y_4	y_5	y_6	y_7	y_8	y_9
M	y_7	350	2	1	2	-1	0	0	1	0	0
M	y_8	300	1	1	1	0	-1	0	0	1	0
M	y_9	400	4	1	2	0	0	-1	0	0	1	$\to$
$\omega_j - \gamma_j$		0	-160	-100	-120	0	0	0	0	0	0
		1050	7	3	5	-1	-1	-1	0	0	0

$\uparrow$

Table 2.7.1.

The simplex of the tables is filled in as usual. Only are the coefficients in row $(\omega_j - \gamma_j)$ divided into two parts. In the first part of the row are entered the coefficients with which M does not occur, and in the second part, the coefficients with which M occurs. So, for example, is the coefficient $(\omega_1 - \gamma_1) = 7M\text{-}160$. It is obtained by multiplying column C, and column y_1, the products are collected, and the coefficient from the header is subtracted. The coefficients for the other columns were determined in the same way.

---

[1]When looking for the maximum value of the criterion function, in addition to artificial pro me neer we introduce the coefficient $-M$.

The division of coefficients from the order $(\omega_j - \gamma_j)$ into two parts is done only for practical reasons. As M is a very large number, it will, as long as are artificial variables in the solution, the second part of the order is determined which variable enters the next solution.

Did the first simplex table find the optimal solution and, if not, which variable should you choose to enter into the next solution? The answer is quite obvious here: the initial solution cannot be optimal. As long as there are positives in row $(\omega_j - \gamma_j)$ coefficients (and we look for the minimum value of the function), not found the optimal solution. Let's add a second criterion to this: next, the solution should be entered by the variable to which in the simplex table corresponds to the highest (positive) value of the coefficient in the order $(\omega_j - \gamma_j)$.

Let's go back to the first table and find that the optimal solution was not found, and that the variable y_1 should enter into the next solution. Based on the quotient between column y_0 and column y_1, from solution output variable y_9. The first simplex table is marked with a column y_1, the third row in which the variable is y_9 and is rounded off characteristic coefficient. Based on the first simplex so prepared tables, we get another simplex table.

The basic solution in the second table is made up of variables:

$$y_1 = 100 \quad y_7 = 150 \quad y_8 = 200$$

and the value of the criterion function is $\omega_0 = 16000 + 350M$. No optimal solution found. The next solution is yes, the variable y_3 will enter, and the variable will come out of the solution y_7. Therefore, in the second table, we marked the column y_3, the first row in which the variable is y_7, and you round off the characteristic coefficient.

			160	100	120	0	0	0	M	M	M	
C	B	y_0	y_1	y_2	y_3	y_4	y_5	y_6	y_7	y_8	y_9	
M	y_7	150	0	1/2	$\boxed{1}$	-1	0	1/2	1	0	-1/2	$\to$
M	y_8	200	0	3/4	1/2	0	-1	1/4	0	1	-1/4	
160	y_1	100	1	1/4	1/2	0	0	-1/4	0	0	1/4	
$\omega_j - \gamma_j$		16000	0	- 60	- 40	0	0	- 40	0	0	40	
		350	0	5/4	3/2	-1	-1	3/4	0	0	-7/4	

$$\uparrow$$

Table 2.7.2.

We compile a third simplex table.

			160	100	120	0	0	0	M	M	M	
C	B	y_0	y_1	y_2	y_3	y_4	y_5	y_6	y_7	y_8	y_9	
120	y_3	150	0	1/2	1	- 1	0	1/2	1	0	-1/2	
M	y_8	125	0	$\boxed{1/2}$	0	1/2	-1	0	-1/2	1	0	$\to$
160	y_1	25	1	0	0	1/2	0	-1/2	-1/2	0	1/2	
$\omega_j - \gamma_j$		22000	0	- 40	0	- 40	0	- 20	40	0	20	
		125	0	1/2	0	1/2	-1	0	-3/2	0	- 1	

$$\uparrow$$

Table 2.7.3.

Even the third simplex table was not found the solution optimally. There is another artificial variable in the solution ($y_8 = 125$), and there are positives in the second part of row ($\omega_j - \gamma_j$) coefficients. It is necessary to determine which variable enters the next solution. We see that in the third simplex table, two variables (y_2 and y_4) equal competition to enter the next solution because they have completed the same coefficients. According to the supplementary criterion, the advantage will be to get the variable that (if selected to enter the solution) gets more value. So let's first divide column y_0 by column y_2 and we determine that the variable y_2, if it enters the next word šhading, get value 250; then divide column y_0 by column y_4 we determine that the variable y_4, if it does, will get 50.

Therefore, the next solution enters a variable that receives a higher value, i.e., variable y_2. In the third table, we marked the column y_2, then the second row (because the variable y_8 comes out of the solution) and rounded off the characteristic coefficient. We compile a fourth simplex table.

			160	100	120	0	0	0	M	M	M
C	B	y_0	y_1	y_2	y_3	y_4	y_5	y_6	y_7	y_8	y_9
120	y_3	25	0	0	1	$-3/2$	1	$1/2$	$3/2$	-1	$-1/2$
100	y_2	250	0	1	0	1	-2	0	-1	2	0
160	y_1	25	1	0	0	$1/2$	0	$-1/2$	$-1/2$	0	$1/2$
$\omega_j - \gamma_j$		32000	0	0	0	0	-80	-20	0	80	20
			0	0	0	0	0	0	-1	-1	-1

Table 2.7.4.

The fourth simplex table has no major variables in the solution. This can be concluded by column B, but also by the second part of row $(\omega_j - \gamma_j)$. Because they are artificial variables solution in this part of row $(\omega_j - \gamma_j)$ below all columns are zero except below the columns of artificial variables where the units with minus sign are.

The problem can still be solved without the corresponding columns ve sta ck variables (these variables once exited solutions, they can no longer return to it) and without another part of the order $(\omega_j - \gamma_j)$. These columns can be ignored immediately as well an artificial variable comes out of the solution. There is, however, the reason to keep these columns: simplex tables provide data that can be used for the analysis of the optimal solution.

Resolve the simplex spreadsheet problem by continuing to estimating the optimality of the solution and choosing the variable to enter the solution takes into account the first part of order $(\omega_j - \gamma_j)$. By watching this of the row in the fourth simplex table, we see that there are no positives coefficients, so we can conclude that the solution is in this table optimally. It consists of variables:

$$y_1 = 25 \quad y_2 = 250 \quad y_3 = 25$$

and the minimum value of the criterion function is $\omega_0 = 32000$.

We said that in the fourth simplex table, the optimal solution was found. However, row $(\omega_j - \gamma_j)$ of column y_4 (column of non-base variable y_4) has a coefficient of zero. This means that we can specify that the variable y_4 enters the next solution and determine another solution with the same the criterion function value. In other words, we can determine another optimal solution, so we need to put together another simplex spreadsheet. As the variable y_4 goes into the next one solution, in the fourth table, we marked the column y_4. From the variable y_1 comes out of the solution, so we also label the third row and rounded off the characteristic coefficient. Now we can specify the fifth simplex table.

			160	100	120	0	0	0	M	M	M
C	B	y_0	y_1	y_2	y_3	y_4	y_5	y_6	y_7	y_8	y_9
120	y_3	100	3	0	1	0	1	-1	0	-1	1
100	y_2	200	-2	1	0	0	-2	1	0	2	-1
0	y_4	50	2	0	0	1	0	-1	-1	0	1
$\omega_j - \gamma_j$		32000	0	0	0	0	-80	-20	0	80	20
		0	0	0	0	0	0	0	-1	-1	-1

Table 2.7.5.

In the fifth simplex table, we get another optimal solution. It is made up of variables

$$y_2 = 200 \quad y_3 = 100 \quad y_4 = 50$$

and the minimum value of the criterion function, $\omega_0 = 32000$, is the same as for the solution in the fourth simplex table.

Let us just mention that the convex combination of the two optimal solutions can be obtained by other, also optimal solutions. The solutions found using simplex tables are basic; all the solutions that can be obtained as a convex combination of basic solutions are not basic.

We denote the optimal solution from the fourth simplex table with y_0^1, and the solution from the fifth table with y_0^2, so we get the following term for convex combination:

$$y_0^3 = qX_0^1 + (1-q)y_0^2 \quad 0 < q < 1$$

where y_0^3 represents the new optimal solution.

The problem in which the constraint system had all the unequal directions of "$\geq$," is subtracted in all inequalities and added. For problems like this have artificial base. Of course, it may not always be the case. If the problem has fewer artificial variables than the number restrictions, then we have an incomplete artificial base. The procedure of solving these problems makes no difference to the procedure already discussed.

Let us now consider the Ref. [43] method for which there is no increase in the dimensions of the problem. We will look at one canonical form (2.3.0.1) of a linear programming problem:

$$\max \omega(y) = \gamma_1 y_{N,1} + \ldots + \gamma_n y_{N,n} + d$$

$$\text{subj. } \alpha_{11}y_1 + \alpha_{12}y_2 + \ldots + \alpha_{1n}y_n - \beta_1 = -y_{B,1}$$

$$\alpha_{21}y_1 + \alpha_{22}y_2 + \ldots + \alpha_{2n}y_n - \beta_2 = -y_{B,2} \tag{2.7.0.4}$$

$$\ldots \quad \ldots \quad \ldots$$

$$\alpha_{m1}y_1 + \alpha_{m2}y_2 + \ldots + \alpha_{mn}y_n - \beta_m = -y_{B,m}.$$

whereby not all $\beta_i \geq 0$, i.e., there is some $i \in \{1, \ldots, m\}$ such that $\beta_i < 0$ but the coefficients γ_i satisfy the optimality condition. Now the corresponding basic solution $y = (0, \ldots, 0, \beta_1, \ldots, \beta_n)$ is not permissible, i.e., does not belong to the set Γ_P. The task we are solving is finding an equivalent a basic admissible problem (2.7.0.4), that is, finding one basic admissible solution. For this we need a dual simplex method.

2.8 Duality in Linear Programming

In some cases, the mathematical model of the basic LP task cannot help find the optimal plan using the simplex method described. In such cases, the reformulation of the primal task LP into a dual-task, by which a solution can be found. There are the following correspondences between the primary and dual tasks:

1. The dual model has as many variables as the primary constraint task; the restrictions on how much the primary task of variables;

2. The free members in the constraints of the primal task become coefficients with variable functions of the criterion (goal) of the dual model, and the coefficients with the variable functions of the criteria of the primal model become free members in the limitations of the dual model;

3. The direction of the inequalities of the dual model is opposite to that of the primal model;

4. If the maximum of the criterion function is required in the appropriate model, in the dual, the minimum is sought, and vice versa;

5. Supplementary variable y_{n+1} receiving which is in the optimal base solution corresponds to the variable y_j in the dual model, with $y_{n+1}y_j = 0, j = 1, \ldots, m$.

6. It corresponds to the real variable y_j of the receiver from the base admissible solution supplementary variable y_{m+j} of the zero-value dual model $y_j y_{m+j} = 0, j = 1, \ldots, n$.

7. The constraint matrix in the primary model is the same as the transposed matrix limitations in the dual model.

We consider the problem of linear programming in standard form:

$$\begin{aligned} \min \quad & \gamma^T x, \\ \text{subj.} \quad & Ay = \beta, \\ & y \geq 0, \end{aligned} \qquad (2.8.0.\ 1)$$

where A is a matrix of type $m \times n$ with the usual assumption rank $(A) = m$. We associate the problem (2.8.0. 1) with the so-called. *dual problem* shape

$$\begin{aligned} \max \quad & \beta^T y, \\ \text{subj.} \quad & A^T y \leq \gamma \end{aligned} \qquad (2.8.0.\ 2)$$

in which the free coefficients of the problem (2.8.0. 1) have become coefficients in the objective function, and coefficients in the objective function of the problem (2.8.0. 1) become free coefficients in the constraint system. Note that for no negative condition is imposed on vector y. The problem (2.8.0. 1) is in the context of duality theory, it calls *the primal problem*. Adding the of the balancing variables the problem (2.8.0. 2) is reduced to:

$$\max \quad \beta^T y,$$

$$\text{subj.} \quad A^T y + s = \gamma, \qquad (2.8.0.\ 3)$$

$$xs \geq 0.$$

Let Γ_P and Γ_D be admissible sets of problems (2.8.0. 1) and (2.8.0. 3), respectively. There is a link between the target recipient and dual target functions:

Theorem 2.8.1. (Poor Duality). *If* Γ_P *i* Γ_D *void sets and if* $y \in \Gamma_P$ *i* $(y, s) \in \Gamma_D$, *then* $\gamma^T x \geq \beta^T y$.

Proof. Since it is valid that $y \geq 0$ and $s \geq 0$ we get:

$$0 \leq s^T x = (\gamma - A^T y)^T x = \gamma^T x - y^\tau (Ay) = \gamma^T x - \beta^T y.$$

The proof is complete. $\square$

The following theorem is fundamental in the theory of duality.

Theorem 2.8.2. (Strong Duality) *If problem* (2.8.0.1) *has then the optimal solution then also* (2.8.0.3) *has the optimal solution i thereby* $\min \gamma^T x = \max \beta^T y$.

Proof. How optimally the problem (2.8.0. 1) is by assuming the theorem solution, that the application of Algorithm 2 to (2.8.0. 1) ends in the final the number of iterations with the optimum basic allowable solution y^*. Let $j_1 < \cdots < j_m$ be indexes of the base and $i_1 < \cdots < i_{n-m}$ indices of non-basic columns in the corresponding simplex table and let is $\alpha_B = [K_{j_1} \ldots K_{j_m}]$, $\alpha_N = [K_{i_1} \ldots K_{j_{n-m}}]$,

$\gamma_B = (\gamma_{j_1}, \ldots, \gamma_{j_m})$, $\gamma_N = (\gamma_{i_1}, \ldots, \gamma_{j_{n-m}})$. Based on previous considerations of the canonical form of the linear problems, the zero type at the zero position contains $-cTx^* = -\gamma_B^T A_B^{-1}\beta$, at positions $j_1, \ldots, j_m$ contain zeros and positions $i_1, \ldots, j_{n-m}$ contains a vector $\gamma_N - \alpha_N^T(\alpha_B^{-1})^T c_B$ which is non-negative due to optimality conditions. Suppose that $y^* = (\alpha_B^{-1})^T c_B$ and s^* defined with $s_B^* = 0$, $s_N^* = \gamma_N - \alpha_N^T(\alpha_B^{-1})^T c_B$. Then $s^* \geq 0$ i

$$\alpha_B^T y^* + s_B^* = \gamma_B, \quad \alpha_N^T y^* + s_N^* = \gamma_N,$$

i.e., solution (y^*, s^*) is plausible. In addition, it is $\gamma^T x^* = \gamma_B^T A_B^{-1}\beta = (y^*)^T b = \beta^T y^*$. As in Theorem 2.8.1 $\beta^T y \leq \gamma^T x^* = \beta^T y^*$, it follows that (y^*, s^*) is the optimal solution to the problem (2.8.0. 3). $\square$

The following theorem follows Karash-Kuhn-Tucker's optimality conditions.

Theorem 2.8.3. (*i*) $y^* \Gamma_P$ *is the optimal solution to the problem* (2.8.0.1) *if and only if there is* $(y^*, s^*) \in \Gamma_D$ *such that* $\gamma^T x^* = \beta^T y^*$.

(*ii*) $y^* \Gamma_P$ *is the optimal solution to the problem* (2.8.0.1) *if and only if there is* $(y^*, s^*) \in \Gamma_D$ *such that* $(y^*)^T s^* = 0$.

Proof. (i) Let $y^* \Gamma_P$ be the optimal solution to the problem (2.8.0. 1). Then by Theorem 2.8.2 the problem (2.8.0. 3) has an optimal solution $(y^*, s^*) \in \Gamma_D$ and it is valid $\gamma^T x^* = \beta^T y^*$.

If there is $(y^*, s^*) \in \Gamma_D$ such that $\gamma^T x^* = \beta^T y^*$, on the basis of Theorem 2.8.1 implies that for every $y \in \Gamma_P$ it holds $\gamma^T x \geq \gamma^T x^*$. How is $y^* \Gamma_P$, this is y^* optimal re problem solving (2.8.0. 1).

(ii) Let $y^* \Gamma_P$ be the optimal solution to the problem (2.8.0. 1). Then according to (i) there is $(y^*, s^*) \in \Gamma_D$ i $\gamma^T x^* = \beta^T y^*$. When we transpose this equality from subtract equality $(y^*)^T A^T y^* = (y^*)^T A x^*$ we obtain:

$$(y^*)^\tau (\gamma - A^T y^*) = (y^*)^\tau (\beta - A y^*).$$

Now from $s^* = \gamma - A^T y^*$ i $\beta - A y^* = 0$ follows $(y^*)^T s^* = 0$.

If it is valid i$(y^*, s^*) \in \Gamma_D$ such that it is $(y^*)^T s^* = 0$, because permissibility y^* i (y^*, s^*) follows:

$$(y^*)^T s^* = (y^*)^\tau (\gamma - A^T y^*) = (y^*)^T c - (y^*)^T A^T y^* = (y^*)^T c - \beta^T y^* = 0,$$

so it follows from (i) that y^* is the optimal solution to the problem (2.8.0. 1). $\square$

The significance of Theorem 2.8.3 is that the following is established equivalence: the vector $y^* \mathbb{R}^n$ is the optimal solution problems (2.8.0. 1) if and only if there are vectors $s^* \in \mathbb{R}^n$ i $y^* \in \mathbb{R}^m$ so that the following conditions apply:

$$A^T y^* + s^* = \gamma,$$
$$A y^* = \beta,$$
$$y_i^* s_i^* = 0, \quad i = 1, \ldots, n, \tag{2.8.0. 4}$$
$$(y^*, s^*) \geq 0.$$

It is obvious that (2.8.0. 4) is also a necessary condition for yes (y^*, s^*) is the optimal solution to the problem (2.8.0. 3). These conditions play out an important role in the so-called primal-dual inner point methods.

The question of the existence of permissible solutions to the primal and dual problems is solved by the following theorem:

Theorem 2.8.4. (i) $\Gamma_P \neq \emptyset$ *and* $\Gamma_D \neq \emptyset$ *if and only if problems* (2.8.0.1) *and* (2.8.0.3) *have optimal solutions.* (ii) *It is valid that* $\Gamma_P \neq \emptyset$. *Then* $\Gamma_D = \emptyset$ *if and only if* $\inf\limits_{y \in \Gamma_P} \gamma^T x = -\infty$.

(iii) *It is valid that* $\Gamma_D \neq \emptyset$. *Then* $\Gamma_P = \emptyset$ *if and only if* $\sup\limits_{(y,s) y \in \Gamma_D} \beta^T y = \infty$.

Proof. (i) If problems (2.8.0.1) and (2.8.0.3) have optimal solutions, it is trivial $\Gamma_P \neq \emptyset$ i $\Gamma_D \neq \emptyset$.

Let $\Gamma_P \neq \emptyset$ and $\Gamma_D \neq \emptyset$ be observed arbitrarily $(y, s) \in \Gamma_D$. Then by Theorem 2.8.1 the objective function is problems (2.8.0. 1) limited from below and, therefore, it follows from Theorem 2.8.2 that the problem (2.8.0. 3) also has an optimal solution.

(ii) Let $\Gamma_D = \emptyset$ and assume the opposite, i.e., that $\gamma^T y \geq M$ for $y \in \Gamma_P$. Then the problem (2.8.0. 1) has an optimal solution and by Theorem 2.8.2 it follows that the problem (2.8.0. 3) also has an optimal and therefore acceptable solution, which is a contradiction.

It is valid that $\inf_{y \in \Gamma_P} \gamma^T x = -\infty$ and we suppose that $(y, s) \in \Gamma_D$. Then by Theorem 2.8.1 $\gamma^T x \geq \gamma^T y$ for each $y \in \Gamma_P$, which is impossible.

(iii) By introducing the shift $y = y^+ - y^-$, $y^+ \geq 0$, $y^- \geq 0$, the problem (2.8.0. 3) is equivalent to the minimization problem:

$$\min \quad (-\beta)^\tau (y^+ - y^-),$$
$$\text{subj.} \quad A^\tau (y^+ - y^-) + s = \gamma, \qquad (2.8.0.\ 5)$$
$$y^+ \geq 0,\ y^- \geq 0,\ s \geq 0,$$

which is dual

$$\max \quad \gamma^T u,$$

$$\text{subj.} \quad Au \le -\beta, \quad -Au \le \beta, \quad u \le 0. \qquad (2.8.0.\ 6)$$

By replacing $y = -u$ dual (2.8.0. 6) becomes:

$$\max \quad (-\gamma)^T x,$$

$$\text{subj.} \quad Ay = \beta, \qquad\qquad (2.8.0.\ 7)$$

$$y \ge 0.$$

Applying (ii) to the dual pair (2.8.0. 5) and (2.8.0. 7) it follows directly that $\Gamma_P = \emptyset$ if and only if $\inf\limits_{(y,s)y\in\Gamma_D} (-\beta)^T y = -\infty$, i.e. $\sup\limits_{(y,s)y\in\Gamma_D} \beta^T y = \infty$. $\square$

Note that from the proof of Theorem 2.8.4 (iii) the conclusion is that dual of the dual problem equal to the primal problem.

Remark 2.8.1. *In Example 2.6.1, $\Gamma_P = \emptyset$ i $\Gamma_D = \emptyset$, which indicates that this is also possible.*

It is valid that $I_1 \cup I_2 = \{1,\ldots,m\}$, $I_1 \cap I_2 = \emptyset$, $J_1 \cup J_2 = \{1,\ldots,n\}$, $J_1 \cap J_2 = \emptyset$, and let $V_1,\ldots,V_m$ be rows $K_1,\ldots,K_n$ columns of matrix A. Then to problem:

$$\min \quad \gamma^T x,$$

$$\text{subj.} \quad V_i^T x = \beta_i, \quad i \in I_1,$$

$$V_i^T x \ge \beta_i, \quad i \in I_2, \qquad (2.8.0.\ 8)$$

$$y_j \ge 0, \qquad j \in J_1,$$

$$y_j \text{ unbounded by sign}, j \in J_2,$$

a dual problem answers:

$$\begin{aligned}
\max \quad & \beta^T y, \\
\text{subj.} \quad & y_i \text{ unbounded by sign, } i \in I_1, \\
& y_i \geq 0, \quad i \in I_2, \\
& K_j^T y \geq \gamma_j, \quad j \in J_1, \\
& K_j^T y = \gamma_j, \quad j \in J_2,
\end{aligned}$$

(2.8.0. 9)

and the analogs of Theorem 2.8.1 and 2.8.2. Dual symmetric problem linear programming:

$$\begin{aligned}
\min \quad & \gamma^T x, \\
\text{subj.} \quad & Ay \geq \beta, \\
& y \geq 0,
\end{aligned}$$

it is given with

$$\begin{aligned}
\max \quad & \beta^T y, \\
\text{subj.} \quad & A^T y \leq \gamma, \\
& y \geq 0.
\end{aligned}$$

From (2.8.0. 8) and (2.8.0. 9) follows that problem is dual with (1.5.0. 3) given with

$$\max \quad \beta^T y,$$

$$\text{subj.} \quad y_i \text{ unbounded by sign, } i \in I_1,$$

$$y_i \geq 0, \quad i \in I_2,$$

$$y_i \leq 0, \quad i \in I_3,$$

$$K_j^T y \leq \gamma_j, \quad j \in J,$$

$$K_j^T y = \gamma_j, \quad j \in \{1, \ldots, n\} \backslash J.$$

2.9 Dual Simplex Method

Consider the linear programming problem to which the LP table corresponds

$-d$	γ_1	$\cdots$	γ_n
β_1	α_{11}	$\cdots$	α_{1n}
$\vdots$	$\vdots$		$\vdots$
β_m	α_{m1}	$\cdots$	α_{mn}

which we call *dual simplex table* if it contains m different base columns and $\gamma_1 \geq 0, \ldots, \gamma_n \geq 0$. If $\beta_1 \geq 0, \ldots, \beta_m \geq 0$, then the dual simplex table is also and a simplex table to which the optimal basic solution corresponds. If there is $k \in \{1, \ldots, m\}$ such that $\beta_k < 0$ i $\alpha_{k1} \geq 0, \ldots, \alpha_{kn} \geq 0$, we have shown that the set of admissible solutions is empty. If there is $\alpha_{ki} < 0$ it is possible to apply the dual simplex method.

Let a linear programming problem be given:

$$\min \quad d + \gamma^T x,$$

$$\text{subj.} \quad Ay = \beta,$$

$$y \geq 0,$$

to which the initial dual simplex table corresponds DT_0 :

$$
\begin{array}{cccc}
-d^0 & \gamma_1^0 & \cdots & \gamma_n^0 \\
\beta_1^0 & \alpha_{11}^0 & \cdots & \alpha_{1n}^0 \\
\vdots & \vdots & & \vdots \\
\beta_m^0 & \alpha_{m1}^0 & \cdots & \alpha_{mn}^0
\end{array}
$$

The conditions for applying the dual simplex method are now fulfilled by the following algorithm:

Algorithm 4. (Dual simplex method).

Put $k = 0$; $k-$ this iteration is followed by the following steps:

Step 1. If $\beta_i^k \geq 0$ for all $i = 1, \ldots, m$, the algorithm stops, because the base admissible solution is optimal.

Step 2. For each i for which $\beta_i^k < 0$, examine whether $\alpha_{ij}^k \geq 0$ for all $j = 1, \ldots, n$. $\dfrac{\gamma_r^k}{\alpha_{sr}^k} = \max \left\{ \dfrac{\gamma_j^k}{\alpha_{sj}^k} | \alpha_{sj}^k < 0 \right\}.$

Step 4. Apply the following elemental transformations to DT_k:

• multiply $s-$th row with $-\alpha_{ir}^k / \alpha_{sr}^k$ and add to rows $i = 0, \ldots, m, i \neq s$;

• divide $s-$th row with α_{sr}^k.

Step 5. Replace k with $k + 1$ and go to Step 1.

The dual simplex algorithm is a maximization for the objective function, which follows from the following theorem:

Theorem 2.9.1. *By applying the elemental transformations from Step 4 Algorithm 4 is obtained from the dual simplex table DT_k dual simplex table DT_{k+1} corresponding to an equivalent problem linear programming. In doing so, $d^{k+1} \geq d^k$.*

Proof. Obviously, using elemental transformations gets LP-tab li ca DT_{k+1} corresponding to an equivalent problem linear programming. In doing so, all the base columns are in $s-$ that the species that had zeros remain basic, and $r-$ this column becomes basic instead of one that had a unit in $s-$. For $j = 1, \ldots, n$ is

$$\gamma_j^{k+1} = \gamma_j^k - \frac{\alpha_{sj}^k}{\alpha_{sr}^k}\gamma_r^k.$$

If $\alpha_{sj}^k \geq 0$, from $\gamma_r^k \geq 0$ i $\alpha_{sr}^k < 0$ follows $\gamma_j^{k+1} \geq \gamma_j^k \geq 0$. If $\alpha_{sj}^k < 0$, by choice r in Step 3 follows:

$$\gamma_j^{k+1} = \alpha_{sj}^k \left(\frac{\gamma_j^k}{\alpha_{sj}^k} - \frac{\gamma_r^k}{\alpha_{sr}^k} \right) \geq 0.$$

Therefore, DT_{k+1} is a dual simplex table. From $\gamma_r^k b_s^k / \alpha_{sr}^k \geq 0$, follows:

$$-d^{k+1} = -d^k - \frac{\beta_s^k}{\alpha_{sr}^k}\gamma_r^k \leq -d^k \quad \Leftrightarrow \quad d^{k+1} \geq d^k$$

which completes the proof. $\square$

Example 2.9.1. Let the problem be given:

$$\min \quad 3y_1 + 2y_2,$$

$$\text{subj.} \quad \begin{array}{rrrrrrrl} -y_1 & +3y_2 & +y_3 & & & & = & -1, \\ -2y_1 & -10y_2 & & +y_4 & & & = & -10, \\ 2y_1 & +4y_2 & & & +y_5 & & = & 8, \\ 3y_1 & -5y_2 & & & & +y_6 & = & 6, \end{array}$$

$$y \geq 0.$$

to which the dual simplex table corresponds

0	3	2	0	0	0	0
−1	$\boxed{-1}$	3	1	0	0	0
−10	−2	−10	0	1	0	0
8	2	4	0	0	1	0
6	3	−5	0	0	0	1

By applying Algorithm 4 with framed pivot elements, we obtain:

−3	0	11	3	0	0	0
1	1	−3	−1	0	0	0
−8	0	$\boxed{-16}$	−2	1	0	0
6	0	10	2	0	1	0
3	0	4	3	0	0	1

from which the dual simplex table immediately follows:

−17/2	0	0	13/8	11/16	0	0
5/2	1	0	−5/8	−3/16	0	0
1/2	0	1	1/8	−1/16	0	0
1	0	0	3/4	10/16	1	0
1	0	0	5/2	1/4	0	1

The corresponding basic permissible solution is $(5/2, 1/2, 0, 0, 1, 1)$ optimum and optimal value of the objective function is $17/2$. Note that in this case, the dual algorithm steps are identical to Algorithm 3.

Note that Algorithm 4 can be applied if a dual simplex table is known. If not, we can construct a simplex table using the following algorithm:

Algorithm 5. (Dual algorithm for arbitrary simplex table).

Step 1. We form an initial LP form table

$-d$	γ_1	$\cdots$	γ_n
β_1	α_{11}	$\cdots$	α_{1n}
$\vdots$	$\vdots$		$\vdots$
β_m	α_{m1}	$\cdots$	α_{mn}

If $\gamma_1, \ldots, \gamma_n \geq is0$, we apply Algorithm 4.

Step 2. If $\gamma_j < 0$ for some j i $\alpha_{1j}, \ldots, \alpha_{mj} \leq 0$, the algorithm stops because it is expensive restrictions inadmissible.

Step 3. Let $\gamma_{j_1}, \ldots, \gamma_{j_q} < 0$.

If $q = n$ we choose $\alpha_{in} < 0$ for the stator element, we apply simplex transformation and we move on to Step 1.

If $q < n$ and if there is $p \in \{j_1, \ldots, j_q\}$ such that it is filled following the condition:

$$\min_k \left\{ \frac{\gamma_k}{\alpha_{ik}} \mid \alpha_{ik} > 0, \ \gamma_k \geq 0 \right\} \geq \frac{\gamma_p}{\alpha_{ip}} \geq 0, \qquad (2.9.0.1)$$

S elect $\alpha_{ip} < 0$ for the stoser element, apply the simplex transformation and go to Step 1. If there are more elements $\alpha_{ip} < 0$ that satisfy the condition (2.9.0.1), we choose the one for which

$$\min\left\{\frac{\beta_h}{\alpha_{hp}}\,\Big|\,\beta_h \geq 0,\ \alpha_{hp} > 0\right\} \geq \frac{\beta_i}{\alpha_{ip}}, \quad \beta_i < 0.$$

If the condition 2.9.0.1 is not met, let it be:

$$\min_k\left\{\frac{\gamma_k}{\alpha_{ik}}\,\Big|\,\gamma_k \geq 0,\ \alpha_{ik} > 0\right\} = \frac{\gamma_r}{\alpha_{ir}}.$$

For this r, we set α_{ir} for the pivot element, apply the simplex transformation, and go to Step 1.

Note that no simplex table generated by the dual algorithm does not correspond to the permissible solution of the primal problem except the last one is at the same time a simplex table. We show that each dual simplex the table corresponds to the permissible solution to the dual problem. Let u dual simplex table DT_k index set of basic columns denote čen with B and let be the corresponding base α_B. by renumbering the column in the associated matrix α_B we can achieve that DT_k corresponds to the following linear programming problem:

$$\min \quad \gamma_B^T A_B^{-1}\beta + (\gamma_N^T - \gamma_B^T A_B^{-1}\alpha_N)y_N,$$
$$\text{subj.} \quad y_B + \alpha_B^{-1}\alpha_N x_N = \alpha_B^{-1}\beta, \qquad (2.9.0.2)$$
$$y_B \geq 0, \quad y_N \geq 0.$$

The problem (2.9.0.2) is the canonical form of the standard linear problem programming relative to the base α_B for which it applies $\gamma_N^T - \gamma_B^T A_B^{-1}\alpha_N \geq 0$. We define (y^*, s^*) sa $y^* = (\alpha_B^{-1})^T c_B$, $s_B^* = 0$, $s_N^* = \gamma_N - \alpha_N^T y^*$. Then:

$$\alpha_B^T y^* + s^* = \gamma_B, \qquad \alpha_N^T y^* + s^* = \gamma_N$$
$$s_B^* \geq 0, \qquad\qquad s_N^* \geq 0,$$

i.e., (y^*, s^*) is a permissible solution to a dual problem. So to each, the dual simplex table corresponds to the permissible solution of the dual. Coordinates the vectors s^* are explicitly given in the table and the vector y^* is calculated from the system $\alpha_B^T y^* = \gamma_B$.

2.10 Elimination of Equations and Free Variables

In the beginning, when we defined the forms of the problem linear programming, we have shown how the general form of linear problems is reduces programming to a standard or symmetrical form. Here we will show how Tucker's can be used tables and variable substitution (**Replace** algorithm) to reduce the general linear programming problem to canonical form. So, let us now consider the general form of the linear programming problem:

$$\max \omega(y) = \gamma_1 y_1 + \ldots + \gamma_n y_n + d$$

$$\text{subj. } \mathcal{N}_i^{(1)} : \quad \sum_{j=1}^{n} a_{ij} y_j \leq \beta_i, \quad i = 1, \ldots, p$$

$$\mathcal{N}_i^{(2)} : \quad \sum_{j=1}^{n} a_{ij} y_j \geq \beta_i, \quad i = p+1, \ldots, q$$

$$j_i : \quad \sum_{j=1}^{n} a_{ij} y_j = \beta_i, \quad i = q+1, \ldots, m$$

$$y_j c \geq 0, j \in \mathcal{J} = \{1, \ldots, s\}, \quad s \leq n.$$

Multiply all inequalities of type $N^{(2)}$ by -1 and introduce additional variables $y_{n+1}, \ldots, y_{n+q}$ as in reducing to the standard form. Formally, we mark the pro men li ve on the left of the table with $y_{B,i}$ and those on the right $y_{N,j}$. This gave us a problem in a form reminiscent of the canonical one.

$$\max \omega(y) = \gamma_1 y_{N,1} + \ldots + \gamma_n y_{N,n} + d$$

$$\text{subj. } \alpha_{11} y_{N,1} + \alpha_{12} y_{N,2} + \ldots + \alpha_{1n} y_{N,n} - \beta_1 = -y_{B,1}$$

$$\alpha_{21} y_{N,1} + \alpha_{22} y_{N,2} + \ldots + \alpha_{2n} y_{N,n} - \beta_2 = -y_{B,2}$$

$$\ldots \quad \ldots \quad \ldots$$

$$\alpha_{q1} y_{N,1} + \alpha_{q2} y_{N,2} + \ldots + \alpha_{qn} y_{N,n} - \beta_m = -y_{B,q}$$

$$\alpha_{q+1,1} y_{N,1} + \alpha_{q+1,2} y_{N,2} + \ldots + \alpha_{q+1,n} y_{N,n} - \beta_{q+1} = -0$$

$$\ldots \quad \ldots \quad \ldots$$

$$\alpha_{m1} y_{N,1} + \alpha_{m2} y_{N,2} + \ldots + \alpha_{mn} y_{N,n} - \beta_m = -0$$

$$(2.10.0.\ 1)$$

The difference is only in the equations $q + 1, \ldots, m$. Assuming that they are assigned additional variables that are identically zero, we get the problem in canonical form. The equivalent Tucker table has the following appearance:

$y_{N,1}$	$y_{N,2}$	$\cdots$	$y_{N,n}$	-1		
α_{11}	α_{12}	$\cdots$	α_{1n}	β_1	$=$	$-y_{B,1}$
α_{21}	α_{22}	$\cdots$	α_{2n}	β_2	$=$	$-y_{B,2}$
$\vdots$	$\vdots$		$\vdots$	$\vdots$		$\vdots$
α_{q1}	α_{q2}	$\cdots$	α_{qn}	β_q	$=$	$-y_{B,q}$

$$(2.10.0.\ 2)$$

$$
\begin{array}{ccccll}
\alpha_{q+1,1} & \alpha_{q+1,2} & \cdots & \alpha_{q+1,n} & \beta_{q+1} & = & -y_{B,q+1} \equiv 0 \\
\vdots & \vdots & & \vdots & \vdots & & \vdots \\
\alpha_{m1} & \alpha_{m2} & \cdots & \alpha_{mn} & \beta_m & = & -y_{B,m} \equiv 0 \\
\gamma_1 & \gamma_2 & \cdots & \gamma_n & d & = & \omega
\end{array}
$$

Let us now consider one such equation (e.g., the last one).

$$
\alpha_{m1} y_{N,1} + \alpha_{m2} y_{N,2} + \ldots + \alpha_{mn} y_{N,n} - \beta_m = -y_{B,m} = -0
$$

If all $\alpha_{q+1,j} = 0$ then this equation is either impossible, so the problem is inadmissible, or identity, so it can easily get out of the way. Now let $\alpha_{mj} \neq 0$ for some j. If we replace the variables $y_{B,m}$ and $y_{N,j}$ are given by:

$$
\begin{array}{ccccccll}
y_{N,1} & \cdots & y_{B,m} \equiv 0 & \cdots & y_{N,n} & -1 & & \\
\alpha_{11} & \cdots & \alpha_{1j} & \cdots & \alpha_{1n} & \beta_1 & = & -y_{B,1} \\
\vdots & & \vdots & & \vdots & \vdots & & \vdots \qquad (2.10.0.\ 3)\\
\alpha_{m1} & \cdots & \alpha_{mj} & \cdots & \alpha_{mn} & \beta_m & = & -y_{N,j} \\
\gamma_1 & \cdots & \gamma_j & \cdots & \gamma_n & d & = & \omega
\end{array}
$$

Obviously, the now independent variable $y_{B,m} \equiv 0$ does not affect the objective function or the conditions. It follows that we can throw out the j table column (2.10.0. 3). This reduced the number of nonbasic variables for 1. We repeat this procedure until the base variables that are zero are completely eliminated. The following algorithm can be described.

ElJed algorithm (Equation elimination)

Step 1. If there are no basic variables identically equal to zero, apply bf NoStandardMax algorithm.

Step 2. Let $y_{B,i} \equiv 0$. Find $\alpha_{ij} \neq 0$. If such does not exist, and if $\beta_i = 0$, eject *and* equation and go to step 1, otherwise STOP. The problem is intolerable.

Step 3. Substitute the variables $y_{B,i}$ and $y_{N,j}$, drop the j column, reduce n by 1, and go to step 1.

Similarly, we eliminate the free variables. If any of the basic variables free, e.g., $y_{B,1}$, its value can always be calculated from the equation:

$$\alpha_{11}y_{N,1} + \alpha_{12}y_{N,2} + ... + \alpha_{1n}y_{N,n} - \beta_1 = -y_{B,1}$$

for arbitrary values of nonbasic variables. So this equation is always satisfied and can be thrown out of trouble. Suppose we have eliminated all basic free variables in this way. Also, suppose it is some non-base variable (e.g., $y_{N,j}$) is free. First, let $\alpha_{ij} = 0$ for each $i = 1, \ldots, m$. If $\gamma_j \neq 0$ then the goal function is unlimited if the problem is acceptable. Otherwise, variable $y_{N,j}$ has no effect on the goal function either, so it can be thrown out.

Now let $\alpha_{ij} \neq 0$ for some $i \in \{1, \ldots, m\}$. We replace the variables $y_{B,i}$ and $y_{N,j}$. After the transformation, the variable $y_{N,j}$ becomes basic, so they are eliminated as in the previous case. According to we have:

ElSl algorithm (Eliminating free variables)

Step 1. If there are no free variables, apply the algorithm **ElJed**.

Step 2. Let the variable $y_{B,and}$ be free. Throw out the *and* equation (type) and go to Step 1.

Step 3. Let the variable $y_{N,j}$ be free. If $\alpha_{ij} = 0$ for every $i = 1, \ldots, m$, go to Step 2'. Otherwise, select $\alpha_{ij} \neq 0$ and go to Step 4.

Step 3'. If $\gamma_j = 0$ is to throw out j-th column, reduce n by 1 and go to step 1. Otherwise, drop the j column, go to step 1 and continue with the algorithm until it is determined that the problem is acceptable or not. If permissible, STOP. The goal function is unlimited.

Step 4. Substitute the variables $y_{B,i}$ and $y_{N,j}$. Now $y_{N,j}$ becomes basic free variable, eliminate it as in Step 2.

A complete algorithm has now been introduced to solve the linear programming starting problem. In the following example, we will show how equations and free variables are eliminated at the same time.

Example 2.10.1. The following table is given:

$$
\tau_0 =
\begin{array}{ccccccc}
y_1 & \boxed{y_2} & y_3 & -1 & & \\
1 & 1 & 1 & 6 & = & -0 \\
1 & 1 & 0 & 1 & = & -y_4 \\
1 & 2 & 1 & 0 & = & \omega
\end{array}
$$

The framed variable is free. Let's choose α_{12} for the pivot element. After changing the variables, you get a table τ_1. By ejecting the species corresponding to the free variable and the column corresponding to zero is given the equivalent table τ_1'.

$$
\tau_1 =
\begin{array}{ccccccc}
y_1 & 0 & y_3 & -1 & & \\
1 & 1 & 1 & 6 & = & -\boxed{y_2} \\
0 & -1 & -1 & -5 & = & -y_4 \\
-1 & -2 & -1 & -12 & = & \omega
\end{array}
\qquad
\tau_1' =
\begin{array}{ccccc}
y_1 & y_3 & -1 & & \\
0 & -1 & -5 & = & -y_4 \\
-1 & -1 & -12 & = & \omega
\end{array}
$$

Note that if we now choose (according to the **NoStandardMax** algorithm) α_{12} for the pivot, we get the optimal the solution.

2.11   Revised Simplex Method

The simplex method works by replacing variables at each step with the objective of increasing (decreasing) the function aim or obtain an acceptable solution. In each iteration, variables are replaced, whereby compute new values of Tucker's table elements. During this repair, a series of divisions is made, which causes a numerical error to accumulate. Because of this, the simplex method fails in cases where a large number of iterations are required. To avoid this, it is necessary to have Tucker table elements they calculate using the starting matrix of problems. This is achieved by the revised simplex method.

We look at the problem of linear programming in standard format (1.5.0. 4). Let one basic be given solution (obtained by solving the system $Ay = \beta$ or the method of eliminating equations) y^*. Let's look now the starting problem in canonical form:

$$\max \qquad (\gamma^*)^T x_N - d$$

$$subj. \quad Tx_N - \beta^* = -y_B \qquad\qquad (2.11.0.\ 1)$$

$$y = (y_B, y_N) \geq 0$$

Let us now denote by n and m the row of nonbasic and basic variables and by τ a matrix of type $m \times n$ which represents Tucker's spreadsheet. The vectors β^* and γ^* are the corresponding free vector and the vector of the objective function u canonical form. The system of equations in (2.11.0. 1) can be otherwise written as $[\tau | I_m] \begin{bmatrix} y_N y_B \end{bmatrix} = \beta^*$. Now write the system $Ay = \beta$ in the form $\alpha_B x_B + \alpha_N x_N = \beta$. From this condition and (2.11.0. 1) we get the direct that:

$$\tau = \alpha_B^{-1}\alpha_N \qquad \beta^* = \alpha_B^{-1}\beta. \qquad (2.11.0.\ 2)$$

So if we know the indices of the base variables $v_{B,1}, \ldots v_{B,m}$ ($y_{B,i} = y_{v_{B,i}}$) can we reconstruct Tucker's spreadsheet using formulas (2.11.0. 2). $\alpha_B = [K_{v_{B,1}} \cdots K_{v_{B,m}}]$ was met.

The objective function $f(y) = \gamma^T x$ can be treated here as an equation, with the addition of an additional variable y_{n+1} so that $\gamma^T x + y_{n+1} = 0$. Now the system matrix has the form $\alpha_\gamma = \begin{bmatrix} A0 \\ \gamma^\tau 1 \end{bmatrix}$ with $y_\gamma = (y_1, \ldots, y_{n+1})$. It is also:

$$(\alpha_\gamma)_B = \begin{bmatrix} \alpha_B 0 \\ \gamma_B 1 \end{bmatrix}.$$

So, if we now apply formulas (2.11.0. 2) for an extended system

$$\alpha_c x_\gamma = \begin{bmatrix} \beta^* \\ d \end{bmatrix},$$

we can completely reconstruct Tucker's spreadsheet.

As we can see, the method of reconstruction of the Tucker table just presented does not accumulate, so this method is more stable than the classic simplex method. However, we notice that at every step, we have to calculate the inverse of the matrix, which makes one iteration of the revised simplex method significantly algorithmic more complex than the corresponding iteration of the classical simplex.

With most test cases (and practice problems that come down to linear programming), system matrices are very sparse (*sparse*), i.e., there are few non-zero elements. Unfortunately, inverse matrices *sparse* matrix in the general case no must be *sparse*. It is even possible to construct an example *sparse* matrices of relatively small dimensions whose inverse is absent not a single zero, and in most cases, the number of zeros is very small. Matrix inversion methods take a very long time, and the inverse matrix requires a lot of memory space.

Also, in the algorithms of the simplex method we do not need to know the whole Tucker table. Enough to know (to reconstruct) individual rows or columns of Tucker's table. Below we describe the method we are in calculating the required part of Tucker's table is reduced only to solving a system of linear equations. Denote the j-th column of the matrix A by $A_{\bullet j}$ and i-th row by $\alpha_{i\bullet}$. To reconstruct a j column, it is sufficient to multiply the corresponding column of the starting matrix by α_B^{-1} that is, the system $\alpha_B T_{\bullet j} = K_{v_{N,j}}$ should be solved. Here we have to solve as many systems as the columns need reconstruct. We only need the **NoStandardMax** algorithm one column and vector β. To reconstruct the *and* th order required we know the *and*-th order of the matrix α_B^{-1} and [5, 43, ?] respectively:

$$\tau_{i\bullet} = (\alpha_B^{-1})_{i\bullet}\alpha_N \qquad (2.11.0.\ 3)$$

The vector $(\alpha_B^{-1})_{and\bullet}$ is determined from the following equation:

$$(\alpha_B^{-1})_{i\bullet}\alpha_B = (I_m)_{i\bullet} \implies \alpha_B^\tau(\alpha_B^{-1})_{i\bullet}^\tau = (I_m)_{i\bullet}^\tau \qquad (2.11.0.\ 4)$$

which also represents a system of linear equations to solve.

Note that, to solve a system of linear equations (2.11.0. 3) and (2.11.0. 4), we use methods such as Gaussian elimination, LR factorization, etc. [37]. We only need to reconstruct the **StandardMax** algorithm in the last row (goal function), which means in each iteration of the **StandardMax** algorithm we need to solve three systems linear equations. In the **NoStandardMax** algorithm in each iteration need to reconstruct one row and two columns. As which we can see, except for the great memory savings (reconstruction using an inverse matrix due to the problem mentioned it makes no sense to implement using the *sparse* representation matrix) is obtained on time as well.

Let us now formulate the **StandardMax** and **NoStandardMax** algorithms "language" of the revised simplex method.

RevBasicMax algorithm (Revised simplex method for basic permissible canonical forms). Form a matrix $(\alpha_\gamma)_B = \begin{bmatrix} \alpha_B & 0 \\ \gamma_B & 1 \end{bmatrix}$ where γ_B is a vector consisting of the coefficients of the objective function with basic variables.

Step 1. Solve $(\alpha_B)_\gamma \beta^* = \beta$ i $(\alpha_B)_\gamma^\tau ((\alpha_B)_\gamma^{-1})_{m+1\bullet}^\tau = (I_{m+1})_{m+1\bullet}^\tau$, reconstruct $n+1$ row of Tucker's table $\gamma^* = ((\alpha_\gamma)_B^{-1})_{n+1\bullet} N_\gamma$.

Step 2. If $\gamma^* \leq 0$ the objective function has an extremum. Otherwise, let $\gamma_j^* > 0$

Step 3. Reconstruct j-th column of matrix τ_γ, i.e., solve system $\alpha_B T_{\bullet j} = K_{v_{N,j}}$. If $\tau_{\bullet j} \leq 0$, STOP. The goal function is unlimited.

Step 4. Calculate:

$$\min_{1 \leq i \leq m} \left\{ \frac{\beta_i^*}{\tau_{ij}} \,\|\, \tau_{ij} > 0 \right\} = \frac{\beta_p^*}{\tau_{pj}}$$

Step 5. Drop the variable $y_{B,j}$ (or vector $K_{v_{B,j}}$) from the database and insert the variable $y_{N,j}$ (i.e., vector $K_{v_{B,j}}$). In other words, substitute $v_{B,p}$ and $v_{N,j}$. Go to step 2.

The following algorithm has not been found in the literature, so it is partially original. However, using the previous algorithm without the following is meaningless, because already in the **NoStandard-Max** algorithm, numerical errors accumulate.

RevNoBasicMax algorithm (Revised simplex method for non-basic canonical forms) *Step 1.* Let be the initial basis matrix B.

Step 2. Resolve $(\alpha_B)_\gamma \beta^* = \beta$. If $\beta^* \geq 0$, apply the algorithm **RevBasicMax**. Otherwise, choose $\beta_i^* < 0$ such that *and* is maximal.

Step 3. Reconstruct the *and* -type $\tau_{and\bullet}$ matrix τ (Tucker's tables). If $\tau_{i\bullet} \leq 0$, STOP. The problem of linear programming is unacceptable. Otherwise, select $\tau_{ij} < 0$.

Step 4. If $i = m$ replace the variables $y_{B,i}$ and $y_{N,j}$ and go to step 2.

Step 5. To reconstruct the j-th column of the matrix τ, i.e., solve the system $\alpha_B \tau_{\bullet j} = K_{v_{N,j}}$

Step 6. Calculate

$$\min_{l>i} \left(\left\{ \frac{\beta_i^*}{\tau_{ij}} \right\} \bigcup \left\{ \frac{\beta_l^*}{\tau_{lj}} \| \alpha_{lj} > 0 \right\} \right) = \frac{\beta_p^*}{\tau_{pj}}$$

Substitute the variables $y_{B,p}$ and $y_{N,j}$ and move to Step 2.

Algorithms for the elimination of equations and free probes can be described analogously. In the end, we again mention the advantages and disadvantages of the revised simplex method.

Advantages:

- The elements of Tucker's table τ are calculated directly on the basis of the matrix A, thus avoiding the accumulation error of the computational operations.

- Since the algorithms of the simplex method does not need the entire matrix τ, but only the individual rows and columns, by the revised simplex method, we only reconstruct those rows and columns and not the entire τ matrix.

Disadvantages:

- Given that at each step, we have to either search for an inverse matrix or solve several (maximum 3) systems of linear equations, the iteration of the revised simplex is much slower than the iteration of the ordinary.

- In ordinary simplex, we used a simple algorithm to replace the pros. This is where it needs to be implemented complex algorithms for solving systems of linear equations or inversion of matrices.

2.12 Cycling Concept and Anti-Cyclic Rules

In 2.4.1 Theorem, we have shown that after each iteration of the **StandardMax** algorithm, the value of the function is either targeted or increased, or it remains the same. In this way, we have "proved" that the same algorithm ends up in a finite number of iterations (since there are finally many basic solutions available). In doing so, we have not considered the possibility of value does not change the function of the target while running the **StandardMax** algorithm. In this case, we have no guarantee that the algorithm will **StandardMax** finish in finite time. The following is an example.

Example 2.12.1. Consider the following linear programming problem in symmetric form:

$$\max \omega = \frac{3}{4}y_1 - 20y_2 + \frac{1}{2}y_3 - 6y_4$$

$$\text{subj. } \& \frac{1}{4}y_1 - 8y_2 - y_3 + 9y_4 \leq 0$$

$$\& \frac{1}{2}y_1 - 12y_2 - \frac{1}{2}y_3 + 3y_4 \leq 0 \qquad\qquad (2.12.0.\ 1)$$

$$\& y_3 \leq 1$$

$$\& y_1, y_2, y_3, y_4 \geq 0.$$

Let's form an appropriate canonical form, Tucker's table, and apply the **StandardMax** 7 algorithm:

y_1	y_2	y_3	y_4	-1		
$\frac{1}{4}$	-8	-1	9	0	$=$	$-y_5$
$\frac{1}{2}$	-12	$-\frac{1}{2}$	3	0	$=$	$-y_6$
0	0	1	0	1	$=$	$-y_7$
$\frac{3}{4}$	-20	$\frac{1}{2}$	-6	0	$=$	ω

$$(2.12.0.\ 2)$$

Should we continue with the **StandardMax** algorithm obtained 6 spreadsheets would be repeated over and over again optimal solution. Notice that in steps 2, 3, and 4, the choice element does not have to be unique.

This is the main reason for the occurrence of cycling. Cycling is most often treated as a rare occurrence that occurs only in artificially constructed examples [64, 55]. However, back in 1977, Kotiah and Steinberg [30] discovered a whole class "cycle" problems. Also, as we will see later, when testing the programs, we noticed the occurrence of cyclization on a number of examples.

In this section, we will look at the rules that are being prevented by cycling. These rights are called *anticyclical rules*.

We'll handle two types of anti-cyclical rules:*Lexicographic Method* and *Bland Rules*.

$$\frac{\alpha_{p,n+1}}{\alpha_{pj}} = \min\{\frac{\alpha_{i,n+1}}{\alpha_{ij}} \| \alpha_{ij} > 0\}.$$

Consider now again the appropriate standard form 2.1.0.2, at to which we will add the vector $\beta^{\prime}$ as a null column to the matrix $A^{\prime}$. Cycling is avoided if p is selected in Step 3 so that instead, the minimum reaches the lexicographic minimum. The modified step is:

Determine $j \in \{1,\ldots,n\}$ for which it is valid that $\gamma_j < 0$. Determine $p \in \{1,\ldots,m\}$ such that:

$$\frac{V_p}{\alpha_{pj}} = \text{lex-min}\left\{\frac{V_i}{\alpha_{ij}} | \alpha_{ij} > 0\right\},$$

Example 2.12.2. *In the case of Tucker's table from the example at the beginning of this section, with the same rule for choosing the index j it follows that $j = 1$, $\alpha_{ij} > 0$ for $i = 1, 2$, $i*

$$\frac{V_1}{\alpha_{1j}} = [0,1,-32,-4,36,4,0,0], \quad \frac{V_2}{\alpha_{2j}} = [0,1,-24,-1,6,0,2,0],$$

so lex-min is reached by $p = 1$, and is the first pivot element of α_{11}. Applying the lexicographic rule further generates pivot elements $\alpha_{22}^1, \alpha_{23}^2, \alpha_{34}^3$, leading to Tucker's table τ_4 with new the value of the target function and cycling is avoided.

Remark 2.12.1. *It is important to note that lex-min is always unique because from the assumption it is $\text{rank}A^{\prime} = m$ implies that there are no two proportional types.*

Let us now prove the correctness of the lexicographic rule.

Theorem 2.12.1. *Let A' be all types in the initial matrix $V_1, \ldots, V_m$ lexicographically positive and let it be in the algorithm* **Standard-Max** *step 3 replaced by step 3.' Then the cycling is eliminated, i.e., the simplex method in finite number iteration comes either to the optimal solution or to the conclusion that the target the function is not restricted from below:*

Proof. We will show first that species V_i^k, $i = 1, \ldots, m$, matrices A' remain lexicographically positive. For $i = p$ it is valid that $V_p^1 = \frac{V_p}{\alpha_{pj}}$ pa $\alpha_{pj} > 0$ i $V_p \overset{lex}{>} 0$ implies $V_p \overset{lex}{>} 0$. For $i \neq p$ it is true that:

$$V_i^1 = V_i - \frac{\alpha_{ij}}{\alpha_{pj}} V_p = \alpha_{ij} \left(\frac{V_i}{\alpha_{ij}} - \frac{V_p}{\alpha_{pj}} \right) \overset{lex}{>} 0,$$

where strict inequality applies based on the foregoing. For $i \neq p$ i $\alpha_{ij}^k \leq 0$ it is valid that $V_i^1 = V_i + \frac{|\alpha_{ij}|}{\alpha_{pj}} V_p \overset{lex}{\geq} V_i \overset{lex}{>} 0$. For $m+1$-th row it is valid that:

$$V_{m+1}^1 = V_{m+1} - \frac{\alpha_{m+1,j}}{\alpha_{pj}} V_p = V_{m+1} + \frac{|\alpha_{m+1,j}|}{\alpha_{pj}} V_p \overset{lex}{>} V_{m+1}$$

because of

$$\alpha_{m+1,j} < 0, \ \alpha_{pj} > 0 \quad i \quad V_p \overset{lex}{>} 0.$$

Therefore, $m+1$ is strictly lexicographically growing and cannot be repeated. □

Remark 2.12.2. *The assumption of lexicographic positivity of matrix types A' in the previous theorem is not restrictive as this can be achieved in to every canonical form of linear programming. It is enough, at the beginning, to perform renumber the variables and bring the columns of the unit matrix to positions $1, \ldots, m$.*

We are reminded that for simpler formulation.

Step 3. Determine $s \in \{1, \ldots, m\}$ for which $\alpha_{s0}^k < 0$. Determine $r \in \{1, \ldots, m\}$ such that $\dfrac{\alpha_{0r}^k}{\alpha_{sr}^k} = \max \left\{ \dfrac{\alpha_{0j}^k}{\alpha_{sj}^k} \middle| \alpha_{sj}^k < 0 \right\}$;

Let's take the following step:

Step 3'. Determine $s \in \{1, \ldots, m\}$ for which it is true $\beta_s^k < 0$. Determine $r \in \{1, \ldots, m\}$ such that $\dfrac{K_r^k}{\alpha_{sr}^k} = \text{lex-} \max \left\{ \dfrac{K_j^k}{\alpha_{sj}^k} \middle| \alpha_{sj}^k < 0 \right\}$,

where K_j^k j–th column k–th of dual simplex table.

We can prove the finality of the dual simplex method.

Theorem 2.12.2. *Let DT_0 columns in the dual simplex table $K_1^0, \ldots, K_n^0$ lexicographically positive and let it be in Algorithm 4 Step 3 replaced by Step 3.' Then the string of zero columns (K_0^k) is strictly lexicographically, the dual simplex method also decreases in the final number iteration comes either to the optimal solution or to the conclusion that the admissible set is empty.*

Let's now consider **Bland's rules**. According to Bland [7], the following two modifications should apply steps 2 and 4:

- *Step 2'. Select $\gamma_j > 0$ such that the index of the corresponding non-base variable is $y_{N,j}$ the smallest.*

- *Step 4'.*

$$\min_{1 \leq and \leq m} \left\{ \frac{\beta_i}{\alpha_{ij}}, \quad \alpha_{ij} > 0 \right\} = \frac{\beta_p}{\alpha_{pj}}$$

In the case of equal values, choose p such that it is an index corresponding base changes like $y_{B,p}$ smallest. Substitute the non-base variable $y_{N,j}$ and the base variable $y_{B,p}$ and go to Step 1. *Calculate*

$$\min_{1 \leq and \leq m} \left\{ \frac{\beta_i}{\alpha_{ij}}, \quad \alpha_{ij} > 0 \right\} = \frac{\beta_p}{\alpha_{pj}}$$

In the case of equal values, choose p such that it is an index corresponding base changes like $y_{B,p}$ smallest. Substitute the non-base variable $y_{N,j}$ and the base variable $y_{B,p}$ and go to Step 1.

Let us now prove the correctness of these rules. In the proof, the matrix A represents the system matrix, vectors β and γ RHS vector and vector objective functions in the appropriate standard problem form, a matrix τ extended Tucker table. These marks are the same as in section 2.11.

Theorem 2.12.3. *Bland rules eliminate cycling in simplex methods.*

Proof. Assume the opposite. Let τ be a set of indexes j such that variable y_j during cycle **becomes** basic. Let it be $q = \max \tau$. Let τ' be a table with variable y_q **becomes** basic a τJ table where y_q **becomes** non-base (in the tables τ' and τJ the variable y_q is non-base and basic respectively). Label it with t pivot transformation column after which we get table τJ.

We define the vectors $y = (y_1, \ldots, y_n, y_{n+1})$ and $v = (v_1, \ldots, v_n, v_{n+1})$ as follows:

$$y_i = \begin{cases} 1 & i = n+1 \\ \tau'_{n+1,j} & i = v'_{N,j} \\ 0 & \text{in contrary} \end{cases} \qquad v_i = \begin{cases} -1 & i = v\text{J}_{N,t} \\ \tau\text{J}_{it} & i = v\text{J}_{B,i} \\ 0 & \text{in contrary} \end{cases}$$

Based on **the first Bland rule**, $y_1, \ldots, y_{q-1} \geq 0$ and $y_q < 0$. Since $\tau = (\alpha_\gamma)_B^{-1}(\alpha_\gamma)_N$. If we rearrange the columns of matrices α_γ and vectors y and v we can write $\alpha_\gamma = \begin{bmatrix} (\alpha_\gamma)_B & (\alpha_\gamma)_N \end{bmatrix}$ as well $v = \begin{bmatrix} \tau_{J \bullet t} & -(I_m)_{\bullet t} \end{bmatrix}^T$ i $y = \begin{bmatrix} \tau'_{n+1 \bullet} 0 \end{bmatrix}^T$.

Now we have that:

$$\alpha_c v = [(\alpha_\gamma)_B (\alpha_\gamma)_N] \begin{bmatrix} \tau_{J \bullet t} \\ -(I_m)_{\bullet t} \end{bmatrix} = ((\alpha_\gamma)_N)_{\bullet t} - ((\alpha_\gamma)_N)_{\bullet t} = 0$$

The signs v belong to the kernel $\mathcal{N}(\alpha_\gamma)$ of the matrix α_γ. Note also that the vector y bass $n+1$ is a vector matrix type $(\alpha_\gamma)_B^{-1}\alpha_\gamma$. It follows that $y^T v = 0$. Note that $v_{n+1} = \tau_{Jm+1,t} < 0$, so $y_{n+1}v_{n+1} < 0$. So there is j, so $y_j v_j > 0$.

Since $y_j \neq 0$, the variable y_j is basic in τ' and since $v_j \neq 0$, or y_j is non-basic in τ_J or $j = t$. In any case, $j \in \tau$, so $j \leq q$. Also, since $v_q = \tau_{Jp_Jt} > 0$ ($q = v_{JB,p_J}$, according to Step 4 of the algorithm **StandardMax** a $y_q = \tau'_{m+1,p'} < 0$ ($q = v'_{N,p'}$, by step 2 of the algorithm **StandardMax**, we have that $y_q v_q < 0$, so $1 \geq j < q$. Since $y_j \geq 0$ it follows that $v_j \geq 0$.

We conclude that the variable y_j is basic in table τ_J. Therefore, let $j = v_{B,k}$. Now $\tau_{Jkt} = v_j > 0$. Note also that during the cycle, the last column of Tucker's table τ (vector β^*) does not change. Namely, since the value of the objective functions $\tau_{m+1,n+1}$ does not change, on the basis of formulas (2.3.0.5) we conclude that $\beta_p^* = 0$ (p is the index of the pivot type), so based on the same the formula doesn't change β^* either.

Values of all variables from τ in the corresponding baselines solutions are 0. Indeed, if $\omega \in \tau$ and y_ω are basic variable, let's notice the moment when it became basic. Then, if the pivot element is τ_{Jql}, where $v_{N,l} = \omega$ i $\beta_q^* = 0$, after transformation we have that $v_{B,q} = \omega$ a β_q^* remains 0.

Therefore $(\beta^*)_{Jk} = \tau_{Jk,n+1} = 0$. So now we have $(\beta^*)_{Jk} = 0, \tau_{Jkt} > 0$, $v_{JB,k} = j$ a $v_{JB,pJ} = q$ where pJ is the corresponding pivot type (in the next iteration y_q becomes non-base). Based on **the second Bland rule**, we conclude that $q = v_{JB,pJ} \leq v_{JB,k} = j$ which is a contradiction. This proves the theorem. $\square$

An example of how these rules avoid cycling in the previous example can be found in Ref. [43].

Let us mention at the end two shortcomings of Bland's rules. Applying these rules may result in such a choice pivot element that changes in the value of the goal function are small, which often causes more iterations simplex method. There is also a danger of picking pivot elements that are close to zero and cause large one's numerical errors.

2.13   Complexity of Simplex Methods and Minty-Klee Polyhedra

In the introduction, we mentioned that despite the good features he showed in practice, the simplex algorithm is not polynomial. This claim was first proven by Minty and Klee in [28], back in 1970, assuming that for the pivot column, the first column is $\gamma_j < 0$. It was later proven to [29] for almost everyone deterministic pivot column selection rule there is a class example of linear programming problems such that the number of iterations the simplex method depends exponentially on the dimension of the problem.

Definition 2.13.1. *Let's look at the following linear programming problem, given in canonical form and via Tucker's table:*

$$\min \epsilon^{n-1} y_1 + \epsilon^{n-2} y_2 + \ldots + \epsilon y_{n-1} + y_n$$

$$
\begin{aligned}
y_1 &\leq t \\
2\epsilon y_1 + y_2 &\leq t^2 \\
2\epsilon^2 y_1 + 2\epsilon y_2 &\leq t^3 \\
&\vdots \\
2\epsilon^{n-1} y_1 + 2\epsilon^{n-2} y_2 + \ldots + 2\epsilon y_{n-1} + y_n &\leq t^n \\
y &\geq 0
\end{aligned}
$$

y_1	y_2	$\cdots$	y_n	-1		
1	0	$\cdots$	0	t	$= -y_{n+1}$	
2ϵ	1	$\cdots$	0	t^2	$= -y_{n+2}$	
$\vdots$	$\vdots$	$\ddots$	$\vdots$	$\vdots$	$\vdots$	
$2\epsilon^{n-1}$	$2\epsilon^{n-2}$	$\cdots$	1	t^m	$= -y_{n+m}$	
ϵ^n	ϵ^{n-1}	$\cdots$	1	0	$= f$	

Label this problem with $\mathcal{P}_n(\epsilon, t)$ and call ita general Minty-Klee problem of dimension n.

In their work [28], Minty and Klee observed the problem of $\mathcal{P}_n(2, 5)$. Obviously, for $t > 0$, this problem is basically permissible, so we can immediately apply the algorithm **StandardMax**. Now let us prove that the algorithm **StandardMax** after $2^n - 1$ iterations comes to an optimal solution $y^* = (0, \ldots, 0, t^n)$ $(y^* \in \mathbb{R}^n)$. This is precisely what the main theorem of this section states:

Theorem 2.13.1. *Let $\epsilon, t > 0$ and $\frac{\epsilon}{t} > \frac{1}{2}$. The algorithm* **Standard-Max***, applied to the problem $\mathcal{P}(\epsilon, t)$, undergoes an $2^n - 1$ iteration to the optimal solutions $y^* = (0, \ldots, 0, t^n)$.*

Before giving evidence, let us consider some features of the general Minty-Klee problem.

Lemma 2.13.1. *Let the conditions of Theorem 2.13.1 apply. If we apply an algorithm to replace variables k times, whereby the pivot elements are $a^i_{p_i p_i} = 1$ where the numbers $p_i \in \{1, \ldots, n\}$, $i = 0, \ldots, k-1$ a with a^l_{ij} is an element of (i, j) of Tucker's table after l transformations, we get Tucker's table of τ_k whose elements are equal to $t^k_{ij} = (-1)^{\gamma^k_{ij}} t^0_{ij}$, for $j < n + 1$. With γ^l_{ij} we denote the number of pivot elements p_s for which $j \le p_s < i$ and $1 \le s \le l$.*

Proof. We will prove the proof by mathematical induction. For $l = 0$, the claim is trivial, given that $\gamma^0_{ij} = 0$ for each $(i, j) \in \{1, \ldots, m + 1\} \times \{1, \ldots, n\}$. Suppose the claim holds for all numbers less than or equal to k and prove it for $k + 1$. Let $p = p_{k+1}$. According to the induction hypothesis, in the pivot type and the p pivot column, the elements are non-zero in sequence t^k_{ip} and t^k_{pj} such that $i \ge p$ a $p \ge j$. Therefore, if at least one of these two conditions does not apply, we have that $t^{k+1}_{ij} = t^k_{ij}$ and $\gamma^{k+1}_{ij} = \gamma^k_{ij}$, because $p \notin [j, i)$ so the claim of the lemma is valid.

For $i = p$ it is valid that

$$. \qquad t^{k+1}_{pj} = \frac{t^k_{pj}}{t^k_{pp}} = t^k_{pj} = (-1)^{\gamma^k_{pj}} t^0_{pj} = (-1)^{\gamma^{k+1}_{pj}} t^0_{pj}$$

because $\gamma_{pj}^{k+1} = \gamma_{pj}^k$, for $j \geq p$. For $j = p$ we have that:

$$t_{ip}^{k+1} = -\frac{t_{ip}^k}{t_{pp}^k} = -t_{ip}^k = -(-1)^{\gamma_{ip}^k} t_{ip}^0 = (-1)^{\gamma_{ip}^{k+1}} t_{ip}^0$$

because $\gamma_{ip}^{k+1} = \gamma_{ip}^k + 1$ for $i \leq p$.

For $j < p$ and $p < i$ is obtained:

$$t_{ij}^{k+1} = t_{ij}^k - t_{pj}^k t_{ip}^k = (-1)^{\gamma_{ij}^k} t_{ij}^0 - (-1)^{\gamma_{ip}^k + \gamma_{pj}^k} t_{ip}^0 t_{pj}^0$$

Since it is $t_{ij}^0 = 2\epsilon^{i-j}$ i $\gamma_{ip}^k + \gamma_{pj}^k = \gamma_{ij}^k$ we have

$$t_{ij}^{k+1} = (-1)^{\gamma_{ij}^k} \left(t_{ij}^0 - t_{ip}^0 t_{pj}^0 \right) = (-1)^{\gamma_{ij}^k} \left(2\epsilon^{i-j} - 4\epsilon^{i-p+p-j} \right)$$
$$= -(-1)^{\gamma_{ij}^k} 2\epsilon^{i-j} = (-1)^{\gamma_{ij}^{k+1}} t_{ij}^0.$$

that $\gamma_{ij}^{k+1} = \gamma_{ij}^k + 1$ because $i > p$ and $p > j$. This proves the lemma. $\square$

From the evidence of the previous lemma it follows that if we always choose the pivot species $p = j$ (select pivot column as in algorithm **StandardMax**) after $2^n - 1$ steps we arrive at the optimal solution. To prove it, suppose in the k th step we selected the j th column for kljucnu. Then $\tau_{m+1,1}^k, \ldots, \tau_{m+1,j-1}^k < 0$ a $\tau_{m+1,j}^k > 0$. Now choosing the element τ_{jj}^k for the key, at on the basis of the evidence of the previous lemma, we conclude that after transformations of vasitis $\tau_{m+1,1}^{k+1}, \ldots, \tau_{m+1,j-1}^{k+1} > 0$ a $\tau_{m+1,j}^{k+1} < 0$. Let us now add one natural number to each Tucker table τ^k $\tau(\tau^k)$ as follows. Digit at l th position in binary notation $\tau(\tau^k)$ equals 0 if $\tau_{m+1,l}^k$ positive otherwise is equal to 1. We just proved that it is valid $\tau(\tau^{k+1}) = \tau(\tau^k) + 1$, or $\tau(\tau^k) = k$. The algorithm stalls when all the digits of the number $\tau(\tau^k)$ are equal to one, that is, when $k = 2^n - 1$.

The following lemma, which we will not prove, ends with the proof of Theorem 2.13.1:

Lemma 2.13.2. *In each iteration of the algorithm* **StandardMax** *applied to the* $\mathcal{P}_n(\epsilon, t)$ *problem* $p = j$, *i.e., the pivot element will be on the main diagonal of the Tucker table.*

The polyhedron of admissible solutions Γ_P for the problem $\mathcal{P}(\epsilon, t)$ is called *Minty-Klee poly edar*. Note that if we make the appropriate shifts of variables, the Minty-Klee polyhedron can also be described by the following by a system of inequalities:

$$
\begin{aligned}
\min \quad & y_n \\
\text{subj.} \quad & y_1 \leq 1 \\
& \epsilon y_1 \leq y_2 \leq 1 - \epsilon y_1 \\
& \epsilon y_2 \leq y_3 \leq 1 - \epsilon y_2 \\
& \quad \vdots \\
& \epsilon y_{n-1} \leq y_n \leq 1 - \epsilon y_{n-1} \\
& y \geq 0
\end{aligned}
$$

Geometrically, the last system represents a deformed n-dimensional unit hypercube.

Minty-Klee polyhedra and their properties have been studied by a number of authors. With repeated repetition of appropriate inequality, it was shown in [19] that a certain class of interior-point method also has exponential complexity at worst. In [20], we have considered a variant of simplex methods in which both pivot columns and pivot species are selected at random. In this case, the expected number of iterations for the example was calculated $\mathcal{P}_n(\epsilon, t)$ which is:

$$G_n(\bar{y}) = n + 2 \sum_{k=1}^{n} \frac{(-1)^{k+1}}{k+2} \binom{n-k}{2} \approx \left(\frac{\pi}{4} - \frac{1}{2}\right) n^2.$$

Chapter 3

Three Direct Methods in Linear Programming

In addition to the classic simplex methods, there are alternative methods for solving problems in linear programming that based on either the geometric properties of the constraint set [10, 16] or on general inverses [47, 45]. We also mention papers relating to Banach premises [31]. We describe the results of a similar type in this chapter and introduce three different methods for solving problems in linear programming that satisfy certain conditions. The first method finds a starting point that represents either an extreme point or an adjacent point extreme point. The second method is based on game theory, and the third method is based on general inverses. In the event that the conditions for finding the extreme point directly are not satisfied, these methods can be applied to construct the initial points for the classic simplex method. Improved efficiency simplex method, with the starting point obtained by applying new one's method, is compared with the original simplex method as well as the method's inner points, as illustrated by several characteristic examples. In addition, the elimination of dependent constraints on the linear programming problem is considered. By the end of this section, we are following the papers [52, 53] and [47].

3.1   Basic Terms

Consider the problem of linear programming in which the constraints are inequalities. Determine the maximum of the linear objective function

$$\omega(y) = \sum_{j=1}^{n} \gamma_j x_j = cx \qquad (3.1.0.1)$$

relative to linear constraints

$$\sum_{j=1}^{n} \alpha_{ij} y_j = r_i y \leq \beta_i, \quad i = 1, \ldots, m$$

$$y_j \geq 0, j = 1, \ldots, n \qquad (3.1.0.2)$$

where $r_i y$, $i = 1, \ldots, m$ scalar product of vectors r_i i y, i

$$\gamma = (\gamma_1, \ldots, \gamma_n), \ y = (y_1, \ldots, y_n), \ r_i = (\alpha_{i1}, \ldots, \alpha_{in}), \quad i = 1, \ldots, m.$$

We consider the following problem: generate a convenient starting point for the simplex method, with the aim of reducing the required number of iterative steps to find the optimal solution. It was obtained a method that is applicable to linear problems programming that is defined without dependent conditions. It turns out that the same method is sometimes applicable to linear programming problems where dependent conditions exist.

Below we introduce the method (the so-called *method of minimum angles*), to speed up simplex methods in some classes of linear problems programming. The worst-case method makes a convenient point for the start of the standard simplex algorithm. That point is the solution linear system obtained after replacing $l \leq n$ electives restrictions with corresponding equations whereby $n - l$ variables equal ce ne with zero. For some linear problems programming a simplex method only if tvr ju is a point selected the optimal solution and the algorithm finishes in just one step. In the worst case, the method of minimal angles gives the topics convex together that is adjacent to the extreme point. This method of minimal angles provides, in certain cases, a significantly reduced number of iterative steps compared to the classic simplex method. In addition to accelerating convergence, the dimension of the problem is reduced for certain types of problems. The basic prerequisite for the successful application of minimum angle methods is yes is to give the problem without any constraints. For these reasons, we also consider the problem of eliminating dependent constraints. One direct method based on game theory is also introduced. Some linear programming problems can be solved to be obtained directly, while some of its problems eliminate the necessary restrictions.

In the fourth section, appropriate algorithms for the introduced ones are developed. Here are the most important details of implementing methods minimum angles in the software package MATHEMATICA.

The effectiveness of the presented methods is shown in several illustrative examples. These examples are also compared with standard simplex method dom as well as with internal point methods.

3.2   Minimum Angle Method

The main idea behind [53] is to improve the choice of initial bases. It is well known that the optimal theme is formed as the intersection of n constraints, where n is the number of variables in the LP. Such n constraints that form the optimal theme should capture the least angles with the objective function.

The following definition is required to describe the minimum angle method.

Definition 3.2.1. *Let $P \subseteq \mathbb{R}^n$ be polyhedron (convex set or cone) defined without any inequalities with:*

$$P : \quad \sum_{j=1}^{n} \alpha_{ij} y_j = r_i y \leq \beta_i, \quad i = 1, \ldots, m.$$

The tangential polyhedron P^0 polyhedra P is defined by the following set of inequalities:

$$P^0 : \quad \sum_{j=1}^{n} \alpha_{ij} y_j = r_i y \leq |r_i|, \quad |r_i| = \sqrt{\alpha_{i1}^2 + \cdots + \alpha_{in}^2}, \ss = 1, \ldots, m.$$

The method presented in the following theorem is straightforward and convenient linear programming problems (3.1.0.1)–(3.1.0.2) are defined as optimal pitch in just one step. We will now describe the main idea of that method. In the event that the problem is linear programming with only two variables, we can apply the graphical procedure for solving [46, 64]. Suppose the restrictive conditions are given by inequalities, each of the corresponding real parts equal to the set of admissible and the set of impermissible points for the given conditions. The permissible points are in the P area, which satisfies all the conditions given. The optimal solution can now be determined by drawing the graph of the modified objective function $\omega(y_1, y_2) = 0$ i by its parallel displacement in the direction of the gradient vector (γ_1, γ_2). The optimal solution is unique if the right one $\omega(y_1, y_2) = \omega_{max}$ passes through only one topic (extreme point) of the permissible area. In the case of a minimization problem, we move the given right parallel in the opposite direction.

It is well known that in the n -dimensional case the theme is admissible polyhedra determines by solving the appropriate system with n equation given by bounding conditions ma. In the following theorems we introduce the criterion for the convenient choice of these equations, which is based on the generalization and formalization of the graphical method. This gives us the main result of this section.

Theorem 3.2.1. [53] *Let the maximization problem of the linear be given programming* (3.1.0.1) - (3.1.0.2) *without any inequalities. Let it is* $P \subseteq \mathbb{R}^n$ *polyhedron defined by* (3.1.0.2). *With* $\gamma = (\gamma_1, \ldots, \gamma_n)$ *we denote the gradient vector of the target function. The vectors* r_i *are defined by* $r_i = (\alpha_{i1}, \ldots, \alpha_{in})$, $i = 1, \ldots, m$. *Consider the set*

$$V = \left\{ v_i = \frac{cr_i}{|r_i|}, \ \ |r_i| = \sqrt{\alpha_{i1}^2 + \cdots + \alpha_{in}^2}, \ \ i = 1, \ldots, m \right\} (3.2.0.\ 1)$$

Suppose that V *contains* l *positive elements, denoted by* $v_{i_1}, \ldots v_{i_l}$.

We distinguish the following cases:

(1) *If* P *is an empty set, there is no solution to the problem.*

(2) *If $l = 0$, then $\omega_{\max} = +\infty$, where $\omega_{\max}$ denotes the maximum value of the objective function $\omega(y)$.*

(3) *If $l \geq n$, let y_0 be the solution of the following system of equations:*

$$\alpha_{i_1,1}y_1 + \cdots + \alpha_{i_1,n}y_n = r_{i_1}y = \beta_{i_1}$$
$$\cdots \qquad \cdots \qquad\qquad (3.2.0.\ 2)$$
$$\alpha_{i_n,1}y_1 + \cdots + \alpha_{i_n,n}y_n = r_{i_n}y = \beta_{i_n},$$

with indexes $i_1, \ldots, i_n$ corresponding to a set of n maximum and positive values selected from the set V. If we denote the optimal point in P by y_P, the following cases can occur:

  (i) *$y_0 = y_P$, or*

  (ii) *y_0 i y_P belong to the same boundary hyper straight polyhedra P.*

(d) *In the event that $0 < l < n$, consider the following system:*

$$\alpha_{i_1,1}y_1 + \cdots + \alpha_{i_1,n}y_n = r_{i_1}y = \beta_{i_1}$$
$$\cdots \qquad \cdots \qquad\qquad (3.2.0.\ 3)$$
$$\alpha_{i_l,1}y_1 + \cdots + \alpha_{i_l,n}y_n = r_{i_l}y = \beta_{i_l},$$

where the indices $i_1, \ldots, i_l$ correspond to positive values $v_{i_1}, \ldots, v_{i_l}$ from V. Basic solution y_0 of problem (3.1.0.1) - (3.1.0.2) is given by $n - l$ variables with zero and resolution l equation from (3.2.0.3)

Example 3.2.1. To illustrate the geometric sense Theorems 3.2.1, consider the following problem:

$$\max \omega(y_1, y_2) = y_1 + y_2$$
$$\text{subj.}(\gamma_1) \qquad y_1/3 + y_2 \leq 1$$
$$(\gamma_2) \qquad y_1 + y_2 \leq 2$$
$$(\gamma_3) \qquad y_1 + y_2/3 \leq 1.$$

The minimum angle is captured between the gradient vector $\gamma = (1, 1)$ *target functions and make* $W_2 \equiv y_1 + y_2 = 2$. *Angles between the vectors* γ *and the real* $W_1 \equiv y_1/3 + y_2 = 1$ *and* $W_3 \equiv y_1 + y_2/3 = 1$ *are identical. If we take two angles between the vectors* γ *and the hyper straight* W_2 *and* W_3, *then the solution* $y_0 = W_2 \cap W_3$ *satisfies* $y_0 = (1/2, 3/2) \notin P$. *Similarly, if we take hyper straight* W_2 *and* W_1, *we get* $y_0 = W_2 \cap W_1 = (3/2, 1/2) \notin P$. *The optimal solution* y_P *is in the dark* $y_P = (3/4, 3/4)$. *However,* y_0 *and* y_P *are common elements on the real* W_2. *Condition* (γ_2) *is dependent. If the condition* (γ_2) *is eliminated, we get* $y_0 = y_P = (3/4, 3/4)$.

Remark 3.2.1. If the polyhedron P is defined without dependent constraints, then the 3.2.1 theorem can be successfully applied. If the system the inequality (3.1.0.2) contains several dependent constraints Ȟowever, it is possible that some of the minimum angles in (3.2.0. 1) are determined by dependent constraints. In this case, it may be that $y_0 \notin P$, so that points y_0 and y_P are not elements of the same hyperlink of P. Of course, in this case too y_0 can be used as a starting point for simplex method, but convergence acceleration is not guaranteed in that case. In fact, for the successful application of Theorem 3.2.1, it is sufficient is that none of the l minimum angles is caught with anyone by a dependent restriction. This provides the motivation for the elimination of dependent restrictions, which is discussed in the next section.

Remark 3.2.2. The method used in the case of $0 < l < n$ is also possible apply also in the case of $m < n$. In that case, proposed the method is a modification of a positive method for constructing a basic one solutions from [8]. Note that [8] is basic problem solving (3.1.0.1)–(3.1.0.2) for which $m < n$ applies, obtained by equating $n - m$ variables with zero and solving m equations.

Remark 3.2.3. The method of minimum angles gives the basic solution that belongs to the same hyperlink as the extreme point. Apart from these significant properties, we emphasize the following significant property of this method. U simplex method all restrictions are used in every step as well you add leveling variables. In minimum angle methods, the number of active restrictions is lower than the standard simplex algorithm. Moreover, with the minimum angle methods, leveling variables are not used. Hence the dimension of the problem is considered with the method of minimum angles, which is significant smaller than the dimension of the corresponding application problem simplex method. So, replacing several iterations of simplex methods with only one application of the minimum angle method, it usually means it reduces the number of operations required and the processing time.

Remark 3.2.4. The work [66] gives a counter-example where Theorem 3.2.1 don't mind. Later in his master's thesis, Wang [65] showed that the example from [66] is incorrect because it contains dependent restrictions; then gave a radical counter-example. That said, based on the papers [42], Theorem 3.2.1 can be used as a successful heuristic to find the starting point of a simplex algorithm or, under suitable conditions, the optimal points of a linear problem. Let us also mention that the work [52] apart from [66, 65] is also cited in [2].

3.3 Dependent Constraints and Application of Game Theory

At the beginning of this section, we introduce several rules for elimination of dependent on ra ni ce nja. These rules are also useful in the case are hearing transformations of the problem (3.1.0.1)–(3.1.0.2) into a form suitable for the application of simplex methods. This section is based on papers [52] and [53].

It is known that Gaussian elimination or QR factorization can be applied to eliminate redundant restrictions [14, 64]. However, the following issues occur jumps.

A. Before applying Gaussian elimination, inequalities must be transformed into appropriate equations. That way, the dimension of the system to which the Gaussian elimination is applied usually very significant increases.

B. What's more, rounding errors and need the number of arithmetic operations is significant in many cases with teas.

C. The Gaussian elimination process is linear only dependent constraints of the equality type. Application of the simplex algorithm usually requires the introduction of supplementary variables. In that in the equivalent form, the constraint matrix A is ordinary full rank, so the problem incomplete rank is not of great importance in practice [71].

Implementation of intrinsic point methods for linear problems large-scale programming usually contains a preparatory phase to eliminate dependent variables and dependent constraints [1]. For example, the preparatory phase of PCx executes several types of elimination of dependent variables and dependent ones restrictions [15].

The preparation phase in PCx is running into problems linear shape programming. The preparatory phase checks the input data with respect to the following elimination rules [15].

Blank Types. If the matrix A has a zero type and a corresponding zero coordinate in vector β, this type can be omitted from considerations.

Duplicate Types. When the matrix type is A (and the corresponding element from constraint vector β) is proportional to another, she may be left out.

Duplicate Columns. When the column of the matrix A is proportional to another column, the two columns can be combined. Inbound unified column variables are either normal or free, hundred depends on whether the column proportionality factor is positive or negative.

Fixed variables. If the variable has zero for the above and lower limits, it is obvious that it is possible here equate the variable to zero and omit the problem.

Single-element types. If *and* are the matrix type A contains only one element α_{ij} different from zero, it is clear that $y_j = \beta_i/\alpha_{ij}$, so that variable can be eliminated from problems. Also, the *and*-that type of matrix A can be omitted.

One-element columns. When α_{ij} is the only element different čit from zero in column j of matrix A, and y_j is free variable, then variable y_j can be expressed via other variables that occur in the *and* type matrix A i eliminate it from the problem. Even if the variable is not free, y_j can be eliminated if its constraints are weaker from the restrictions that follow from the domain of the other elements that figure in the form α_i. A similar technique was used in [1]. However, some of the dependent restrictions are not covered by the considerations described u [1] and [15]. As noted in [1], in the case of linear programming problems, the dimension cannot eliminate all the inequalities manually. Thus, the analysis of the preparatory phase aims at improvement problem formulations. To this end, we propose a few additional rules in this section to eliminate redundant restrictions. The first rule is based on the almost sharp geometric properties of some dependent boundaries ăppreciates.

Consider the following limitations with respect to (3.1.0.2):

$$\frac{1}{\beta_i} r_i y = \sum e_{ij} y_j \leq 1, \quad i = 1, \ldots, m$$
$$y_j \geq 0, \quad j = 1, \ldots, n. \qquad (3.3.0.\ 1)$$

where $e_{ij} = \dfrac{\alpha_{ij}}{\beta_i}$, $\beta_i \neq 0$, $i = 1, \ldots, m$, $j = 1, \ldots n$. If it is condition

$$(\exists p, q)(1 \leq p, q \leq m) \ e_{ps} \geq e_{qs}, \quad s = 1, \ldots, n, \qquad (3.3.0.\ 2)$$

satisfied, then q-this limit not from (3.3.0.1) (respectively (3.1.0.2)) may be omitted.

However, this rule of elimination is not universal. For example, depending on the constraint not (γ_2) from the problem (3.2.1) does not satisfy the condition (3.3.0.2).

In the following theorem, a well-known result from game theory is applied, and several additional rules for elimination are defined as a well direct method for solving some types of linear programming problems.

Theorem 3.3.1. *[53] Consider the following linear programming problem: from edit the maximum of the objective function*

$$with(y) = \sum_{j=1}^{n} c_j x_j = cx, \quad \gamma_j > 0, \quad j = 1, \ldots, n$$

in relation to restrictions

$$\sum_{j=1}^{n} a_{ij} y_j = r_i y \leq \beta_i, \quad \beta_i > 0, \quad i = 1, \ldots, m, \quad (3.3.0. \ 3)$$

$$y_j \geq 0, \quad j = 1, \ldots, n.$$

Suppose it is valid $d_{ij} = \dfrac{\alpha_{ij}}{\beta_i c_j}$, $i = 1, \ldots, m$, $j = 1, \ldots, n$. Then the following statements apply:

(1)*In case*

$$\max_{1 \leq i \leq m} \min_{1 \leq j \leq n} d_{ij} = \min_{1 \leq j \leq n} \max_{1 \leq i \leq m} d_{ij} = d_{kl}, \quad (3.3.0. \ 4)$$

the optimal solution to the problem $(3.1.0.1) - (3.1.0.2)$ is

$$y_j = \begin{cases} \dfrac{\beta_k}{\alpha_{kl}}, & j = l, \\ 0, & j \neq l. \end{cases} \quad (3.3.0. \ 5)$$

(2) *If*

$$\max_{1 \leq i \leq m} \min_{1 \leq j \leq n} d_{ij} \neq \min_{1 \leq j \leq n} \max_{1 \leq i \leq m} d_{ij}$$

and if there are k, l such that $d_{ik} \geq d_{il}$, and, $\ldots, m$, then it pulls that $y_k = 0$, so that we can omit the k column.

Also, if there are k, l such that $d_{kj} \leq$ is valid d_{lj}, $j = 1, \ldots, n$, then we can omit the k type.

Proof. Let $y_j = \gamma_j x_j$, $j = 1, \ldots, n$. Then there is the problem (3.3.0.3) is equivalent to the problem $\omega(y) = \sum_{j=1}^{n} y_j \to max$ with restrictions

$$\sum_{j=1}^{n} d_{ij} y_j \leq 1, \quad i = 1, \ldots, m, \quad y_j \geq 0, \quad j = 1, \ldots, n.$$

Note that this linear programming problem is equivalent to playing two players with a payment matrix $D = \|d_{ij}\|$ [39, 53]. Denote the optimal strategy for the other players vector $q = (q_1, \ldots, q_n)$.

(1) If the condition (3.3.0.4) is satisfied, then the optimal strategy for another player pure strategy $q_l = 1$, $q_j = 0$, $j <> l$. How is $\gamma_j x_j = y_j = \dfrac{q_j}{v}$, where is *to* game value, we get [39] $y_j = 0$, $j \neq l$ i

$$y_l = \max_{1 \leq i \leq m} \left\{ \frac{\alpha_{il}}{\beta_i} \right\} = \min_{1 \leq i \leq m} \left\{ \frac{\beta_i}{\alpha_{il}} \right\} = \frac{\beta_k}{\alpha_{kl}}.$$

(2) If k, l such that $d_{ik} \geq d_{il}$, $i = 1, \ldots, m$, then from game theory follows $q_k = 0$, hundred drag $y_k = 0$ [39]. So, we can omit k-th column. If there are k, l such that $d_{kj} \leq d_{lj}$, $j = 1, \ldots, n$, then

$$\sum_{j=1}^{n} d_{lj} x_{ij} \leq 1 \Rightarrow \sum_{j=1}^{n} d_{kj} x_{ij} \leq 1, \text{ for arbitrary} x_{ij} > 0, \ j = 1, \ldots, n$$

such that k-this limit is dependent. $\square$

General Theorems 3.3.1 can be found in [65].

Remark 3.3.1. If all redundant constraints are eliminated, then the condition is $y_0 \in P$ filled. Unfortunately, the proposed algorithms for eliminating redundant restrictions does not guarantee complete elimination. For example, the dependent constraint (γ_2) on the problem (3.2.1) remains after all eliminations. In that case, the basic solution is constructed using the method use minimal angles as a starting point for applying the simplex algorithm.

3.4   Algorithms and Implementation Details

In accordance with Theorem 3.2.1 we introduce two algorithms, denoted by Algorithm An and Algorithm Al for implementing minimum angle methods. These algorithms can be used to maximize the objective function (3.1.0.1) under restrictions (3.1.0.2), and they are possible to apply in the case of $l \geq n$.

An algorithm

Step 1. Eliminate redundant restrictions, using the results in the previous section and Gaussian elimination.

Step 2. Calculate values $v_i = |\gamma| \cos(\gamma, r_i) = \dfrac{\gamma r_i}{|r_i|}$, $i = 1, \ldots, m$.

Step 3. Determine n maximum and positive values

$$v_{i_1} \geq \cdots \geq v_{i_n} > 0$$

from set $\{v_1, \cdots v_m\}$.

Step 4. Calculate y_0 as a solution of the system of equations (3.2.0.2).

Step 5. Check that y_0 is basic admissible solution ($y_1 \geq 0, \ldots, y_n \geq 0$), because implementation of simplex methods in the next step.

Step 6. If the condition is from the previous step filled in, apply the simplex method algorithm *SimMax* from of Section 1.2 for the basic admissible solution [64]). Otherwise, apply the simplex method preparatory algorithm *PreSim Max* from Section 1.2, which generates the first base word ånd complete the algorithm for basic permissible solution [64].

Some software details of*Algorithm An* implementation are described below. The internal form of the problem posed in (3.1.0.1) contains two different parts. The first part is an arbitrary target function, determined by the corresponding an expression from the MATHEMATICA package, denoted by a parameter *objective*. The second part is a list of selected restrictions that we call *constraints*. According to the internal linear form programs required in*functions LinearProgramming, ConstrainedMin,* and *ConstrainedMax* from MATHEMATICA [67, 69], we omit the list of variables used in the target function and the constraints given. The list of variables we omit for ease of use. That list is can be reconstructed using the standard *Variablesfunction* and *Union* (see [68] and [69] for these functions). For this purpose, we define the following function that extracts the list *lis_*.

3.5 Direct Heuristic Algorithm with General Inverses

In this section, we give an algorithm from [47]. This heuristic method very often gives either the optimal or the solution from which, using the simplex method, obtains the optimal solution by applying a small number of iterations. The basic idea of this method is to show the general solutions of the linear system $Ay = \beta$ by *pseudoinverse* $A^\dagger$ (Moore-Penrose general inverse) matrices A. More about the Moore-Penrose inverse as well as other general (generalized) inverses operator and matrix can be found in the monographs [4]. Let's just say it is matrix $A^\dagger$ unique solution of the following system of matrix equations:

$$AXA = A, \quad XAX = y, \quad (Ay)^* = Ay, \quad (XA)^* = XA$$

Other general inverses of the A matrix are similarly defined. There are several methods for calculating Moore-Penrose and other generalized matrix inverses. A method known in the literature as the Leverrier-Faddev or Souriau-Frame method uses the characteristic polynomial of the matrix A. This method is primarily intended for symbolic purposes calculation of general inverses. In [48], a modification of the method Leverrier-Faddev is examined, if the matrix A is a polynomial matrix. Let's also mention the partitioning method in which the Moore-Penrose inversion is calculated using appropriate recurrent formulas. Modifications to this method for polynomial matrices of one or more variables are shown in the papers [44].

We consider the problem of linear programming in standard form:

$$\begin{aligned} \min \quad & \gamma^T x, \\ \text{subj.} \quad & Ay = \beta, \\ & y \geq 0. \end{aligned} \qquad (3.5.0.\ 1)$$

The algorithm input is A, β, γ while the output is vector y, the value of the objective function ω, and the comments based on the optimality test. **Algoritam D2.**

Step 1. Load m, n, $A = [\alpha_{ij}]$, β, γ.

Step 2. Calculate $d = A^\dagger \beta$, where $d = [d_i]$ is the vector of dimension $n \times 1$ a $A^\dagger$ is a Moore-Penrose inverse (or p -inverse) and let $e = Ad$.

If $e \neq \beta$, the output is "The problem is intolerable" and the algorithm stalls.

Step 3. Calculate

$$W = A^\dagger A,$$

$$\gamma' = (I - W)\gamma,$$

$$s_k = \min\left\{ \frac{d_i}{\gamma'_i} \,\middle|\, \gamma'_i > 0 \right\},$$

$$y = d - \gamma' s_k,$$

where $\gamma' = [\gamma'_i]$ $n \times 1$ vector, I is $n \times n$ unit matrix, W is $n \times n$ matrix. The direction vector $\gamma' s_k$ tries to make the vector y move from set of solutions of equation $Ay = \beta$ to set of permissible solutions defined by $Ay = \beta$, $y \geq 0$ if he is no longer in it. The solution will be the extreme point of the set of permissible solutions.

Step 4. Remove that unknown y_i that equals zero, remove *and* column of the matrix A and the corresponding coordinate γ_i from the vector γ of the objective function. Calculate $d = A^\dagger \beta$.

Remark 3.5.1. *The following matrix $A^\dagger$ in Step 4 was calculated from the previous $A^\dagger$. This calculation requires a $O(mn)$ operation. It is possible to calculate A^+ from A, but this requires a $O(mn^2)$ oper-*

ation. If two or more coordinates y_i equate to zero, one should apply the algorithm by eliminating one y_i and compute the corresponding vector y. The vector y that gives the minimum of the objective function of the solution (output) of the algorithm will be sought. There is no suitable criterion for deciding which of two (or more) coordinates of y_i that equals zero will be dropped from the base. However, such a situation is not so common.

Step 5. Repeat Steps 3 and 4 until $s_k = 0$ or cannot be calculated (i.e., $\gamma_i' \leq 0$ for every i).

Step 6. Calculate the value of the objective function $\omega = \gamma^T x$ where they are y and γ obtained in the last step of the algorithm and throw out the result.

Optimality Test. Let be the vector we get using the algorithm, and let A, β, and γ from (3.5.0. 1) be known. Let B be a basic matrix that consists of columns of matrix A corresponding to the basic coordinates y_i vectors y, let γ_B^T be a vector consisting of the coordinates of the vector γ which correspond to the basic coordinates of the y_i vector y, and let p_j j be that column of a nonbasic column of A.

Step 7. Calculate $y^T = \gamma_B^T B^{-1}$ (species vector).

Step 8. Compute $\omega_j - \gamma_j = y^T p_j - \gamma_j$ for all nonbasic vectors p_j.

Step 9. If $\omega_j - \gamma_j \leq$ *is* 0 for every j, then the solution is optimal; otherwise, the solution is unlimited, or the algorithm cannot determine the optimal solution. In this case, the optimal solution is obtained by applying a simplex algorithm using the vector y as a valid starting point.

D2 algorithm comment.

In Step 1, we load the data. Step 2 checks the agreement of the equations $Ay = \beta$. In the case of $e = AA^\dagger\beta \neq \beta$, the problem has no acceptable solution. The general solution of $Ay = \beta$ is $y = A^\dagger\beta \pm Pz$, where $P = (I - AA^\dagger)$ an orthogonal projection operator that projects an arbitrary vector ω orthogonally to null space of matrix A. We calculate the point γ' in the null space of the matrix A in Step 3. The vector $y = d - \gamma's_k = A^\dagger\beta - (I - A^\dagger A)cs_k$ is the form $A^\dagger\beta - Pz$. where cs_k corresponds to an arbitrary vector column ω. Scalar s_k is calculated in Step 3 this way for two reasons:

(i) one (or more) coordinates of $y_a nd$ vectors y are equal to zero,

(ii) the value of the objective function decreases.

In addition, the vector y moves to the set of admissible solutions, if it is not already in it. Sometimes (quite rarely), it happens that the base coordinate equals zero and is marked as non-base. A problem has been opened under which the necessary and sufficient conditions cannot happen.

In Step 4, the variables y_i are eliminated, which equals zero. In numerical experiments, in more than 95 % of the problems, such coordinates are nonbasic.

In Step 5 we check the criterion for the end of the algorithm, while in Step 6, we provide output. In Steps 7, 8, and 9, we check that the solution is optimal. Most often, the matrix is B square and insignificant, and in this case, we check the optimality of the solution directly.

If the matrix B is rectangular $(m < n)$, then we add one (or more) types to the matrix B and one (or more) corresponding elements to vector β such that the newly acquired matrix B and the vector β does not change the vector y and, in doing so, B is a square non-singular matrix. Then apply the optimality test as in Steps 7, 8, and 9. If not $\omega_j - \gamma_j \leq 0$ for every j, let's apply a simplex algorithm using y as a starting point.

Bibliography

[1] Andersen, E. D., Gondzio, J., Meszaros, C., & Xu, X., (1996). *Implementation of Interior Point Methods for Large Scale Linear Programming*. Technical report, HEC, Universite de Geneve.

[2] Angel, S. P., & Pablo, G. G., (2001). *Solving a Sequence of Sparse Compatible Systems*. 19th biennial conf. numerical analysis, Dundee, Scotland.

[3] Bertsimas, D., & Tsitsiklis, J. N., (1997). *Introduction to Linear Optimization*. Athena Scientific, Belmont, Massachusetts.

[4] Ben-Israel, A., & Greville, T. N. E., (2003). *Generalized Inverses: Theory and Applications* (2nd edn., Vol. 15). CMS Books in Mathematics/Ouvrages de Mathmatiques de la SMC, Springer-Verlag, New York.

[5] Bhatti, M. A., (2000). *Practical Optimization with Mathematica Applications*. Springer Verlag, Telos.

[6] Bixby, R., (1992). Implementing the simplex method: The initial basis. *ORSA Journal on Computing, 4*, 267–284.

[7] Bland, R. G., (1977). New finite pivoting rules for the simplex method. *Mathematics of Operations Research, 2*, 103–107.

[8] Bounday, B. D., (1984). In: Edvard, A., *Basic Linear Programming*. Baltimore.

[9] Charnes, A., (1952). Optimality and degeneracy in linear programming. *Econometrica, 20*(2).

[10] Conn, A. R., (1976). Linear programming via a nondifferentiable penalty function. *SIAM J. Numer. Anal., 13*(1), 145–154.

[11] Cormen, T. H., Leiserson, C. E., Rivest, R. L., & Stein, C. (2009). *Introduction to algorithms.* MIT Press.

[12] Chankong, V., & Haimes, Y. *Multiobjective decision making: Theory and methodology Series, Volume 8,* North-Holland, New York, Amsterdam, Oxford, 1983.

[13] Cvetkovic, D., Cangalovic, M., Dugosija, D. J., Kovacevic-Vujcic, V., Simic, S., & Vuleta, J., (1996). *Combinatorial Optimization,* Drustvo operacionih istrazivaca Jugoslavije DOPIS, Beograd. In Serbian.

[14] Cvetkovic, D., (1996). *Discrete Mathematics.* Prosveta, Nis. In Serbian.

[15] Czyzyk, J., Mehrotra, S., & Wright, S. J., (1996). *PCx User Guide,* (pp. 1–21). Optimization technology center, Technical Report 96/01.

[16] Dantzig, G. B., (1949). Programming of interdependent activities, mathematical model. *Econometrica, 17,* 200–211.

[17] Das, I., & Dennis, J. E. (1997). A closer look at drawbacks of minimizing weighted sums of objectives for Pareto set generation in višekriterijumska optimizacija problems, *Struct. Optim. 14* 63–69.

[18] Dax, A., (1988). Linear programming via least squares. *Linear Algebra and its Applications, 111,* 313–324.

[19] Deza, A., Nematollahi, E., & Terlaky, T., (2004). *How Good are Interior Point Methods? Klee-Minty Cubes Tighten Iteration-Complexity Bounds.* AdVOL-Report #2004/20 Advanced Optimization Laboratory, Department of Computing and Software, McMaster University, Hamilton, Ontario, Canada.

[20] Gartner, B., Henk, M., & Ziegler, G. M., (1998). Randomized simplex algorithms on Klee-minty cubes. *Combinatorica, 18,* 349–372.

[21] Gondzio, J., (1995). HOPDM (Version 2.12), A fast LP solver based on a primal-dual interior-point method. *European Journal of Operations Research, 85,* 221–225.

[22] Hitchcock, G. L., (1941). The distribution of a product from several sources to numerous localities. *Journal Math. Phys.*, *20*, 224–230.

[23] Hwang, C. L. & Yoon, K. (1981). Multiple attribute decision making methods and applications: a state-of-the-art survey. In: Beckmann, M., & Kunzi, H. P. (eds.) *Lecture Notes in Economics and Mathematical Systems, No. 186*. Berlin: Springer-Verlag.

[24] Hobbs, B. F. (1980). A comparison of weighting methods in power plant siting., *Decis. Sci.*, *11* 725–737.

[25] Ivanovic, V., (1940). Pravila za proracun potrebnog broja transportnih sredstava, *Vojno-Izdavacki Glasnik, Sveska* 1–10.

[26] Kantorovich, L. V., (1939). *Matematicheskie Metodi v Organizacii I Planirovanii Proizvodstva*. In Russian. Izd. LGU.

[27] Khachian, L. G., (1979). A Polynomial algorithm in linear programming. *Doklady Akademii Nauk SSSR, 244*(5), 1093–1096.

[28] Klee, V., & Minty, G. L., (1972). How good is the simplex method? In: Shisha, O., (ed.), *Inequalities III* (pp. 159–175). Academic Press, New York.

[29] Klee, V., & Kleinschmidtm, P., (1987). The d-step conjecture and its relatives. *Math. Operations Research, 12*, 718–755.

[30] Kotiah, T. C. T., & Steinberg, D. I., (1977). Occurrences of cycling and other phenomena arising in a class of linear programming models. *Communications of the ACM, 20*, 107–112.

[31] Kulkarni, S. G., & Sivakumar, K. C., (1995). Applications of generalized inverses to interval linear programs in Hilbert spaces, *Numer. Funct. Anal. Optimiz., 16*(7/8), 965–973.

[32] Lukovic, M., Lukovic, V., Belca, I., Kasalica, B., Stanimirovic, I., & Vicic, M., (2016). LED-based Vis-NIR spectrally tunable light source-the optimization algorithm. *Journal of the European Optical Society-Rapid Publications*, 12–19, doi: 10.1186/s41476-016-0021-9.

[33] Maeder, R. (1996). *Programming in Mathematica, Third Edition,* Redwood City, California: Adisson-Wesley.

[34] Marler, R.T. (2004). Survey of multi-objective optimization methods for engineering, *Struct. Multidisc. Optim. 26,* 369–395.

[35] Miettien, K.*Nonlinear Multiobjective Optimization,* Kluver Academic Publishers, Boston, London, Dordrecht, 1999.

[36] Miettinen, K., & Kirilov, L. (2005). Interactive reference direction approach using implicit parametrization for nonlinear multiobjective optimization. *Journal of Multi-Criteria Decision Analysis, 13*(2–3), 115–123.

[37] Milovanovic, G. V., (1991). *Numerical Analysis I Part.* Naucna knjiga, Beograd, In Serbian.

[38] Oliveira, V., & Pinho, P. (2010). Evaluation in urban planning: Advances and prospects. *Journal of Planning Literature, 24*(4), 343–361.

[39] Owen, G., (1968). *Game Theory.* W.B. Saunders Company, Philadelphia, London, Toronto.

[40] Nering, E., & Tucker, A., (1993). *Linear Programs Related Problems: A Volume in the Computer Science and Scientific Computing Series.* Elsevier.

[41] Pan, P. Q. (1990). Practical finite pivoting rules for the simplex method. *Operations-Research-Spektrum, 12*(4), 219–225.

[42] Pan, P. Q., (1991). A simplex-like method with bisection for linear programming. *Optimization, 22,* 717–743.

[43] Petkovic, M. D., Stanimirovic, P. S., & Stojkovic, N. V., (2002). Two modifications of the revised simplex method. *Matematicki Vesnik, 54,* 163–169.

[44] Petkovic, M. D., & Stanimirovic, P. S., (2005). Symbolic computation of the Moore-Penrose inverse using the partitioning method. *International Journal of Computer Mathematics, 82,* 355–367.

[45] Pyle, L. D., (1977). *The Weighted Generalized Inverse in Nonlinear Programming-Active set Selection using a Variable-Metric Generalization of the Simplex Algorithm.* Lecture notes in economics and mathematical system, Austin, Texas.

[46] Sakarovitch, M., (1983). *Linear Programming.* Springer-Verlag, New York.

[47] Sen, S. K., & Ramful, A., (2000). A direct heuristic algorithm for linear programming, *Proc. Indian Acad. Sci. (Math. Sci.), 110*(1), 79–101.

[48] Stanimirovic, P. S., & Petkovic, M. D., (2006). Computation of generalized inverses of polynomial matrices by interpolation. *Appl. Math. Comput., 172*(1), 508–523.

[49] Stanimirovic, P. S., & Milovanovic, G. V., (2002). Programming Package Mathematica and Applications, Elektronski fakultet u Nisu, Edicija monografije, Nis. In Serbian.

[50] Stefanovic-Marinovic, J., Petkovi c, M., & Stanimirovi c, I., (2015). Application of the ELECTRE method to planetary gear train optimization. *Journal of Mechanical Science and Technology, 29*(2), 647–654.

[51] Stefanovic- Marinovic, J., Petkovic, M., Stanimirovic, I., & Milovančevi c, M., (2011). A model of planetary gear multicriteria optimization. *Transactions of Famena,* 35(4), 21–34.

[52] Stojkovic, N. V., & Stanimirovic, P. S., (1999). On elimination of excessive constraints in linear programming. *SYMOPIS,* 207–210.

[53] Stojkovic, N. V., & Stanimirovic, P. S., (2001). Two direct methods in linear programming. *Europ. J. Oper. Res., 131*(2), 417–439.

[54] Stojkovic, N. V., Stanimirovic, P. S., & Petkovic, M. D. (2009). Modification and implementation of two-phase simplex method. *International Journal of Computer Mathematics, 86*(7), 1231–1242.

[55] Strayer, J. K. (2012). *Linear programming and its applications.* Springer Science Business Media.

[56] Tasic, M., Stanimirovic, P. S., Stanimirovic, I. P., Petkovic, M. D., & Stojkovic, N. V., (2005). Some useful MATHEMATICA teaching examples. *Facta Universitatis (Nis) Series Electronics and Energetics, 18*(2), 329–344.

[57] Stanimirovic, P., & Stanimirovic, I., (2008). Implementation of polynomial multi-objective optimization in MATHEMATICA. *Structural and Multidisciplinary Optimization, 36*, 411–428.

[58] Stanimirovic, I., (2013). Successive computation of some efficient locations of the weber problem with barriers. *Journal of Applied Mathematics and Computing, 42*, 193–211.

[59] Stanimirovic, I., (2012). Compendious lexicographic method for multi-objective optimization. *Facta Universitatis (Niš) Ser. Math. Inform., 27*(1), 55–66.

[60] Stanimirovic, I., Zlatanovic, M., & Petkovic, M., (2011). On the linear weighted sum method for multi-objective optimization. *Facta Universitatis (Niš) Ser. Math. Inform., 26*, 47–62.

[61] Stanimirovic, I., Petkovic, M., Stanimirovic, P., & Ciric, M., (2009). Heuristic algorithm for single resource constrained project scheduling problem based on the dynamic programming. *YUJOR, 19*, 281–298.

[62] Vanderbei, R. J., (1994). *LOQO: An Interior-Point Code for Quadratic Programming, Technical Report SOR-94-15*. Department of Civil Engineering and Operations Research, Princeton University, Princeton, N.J.

[63] Voogd, H. (1983). *Multicriteria Evaluation for Urban and Regional Planning*, London: Pion.

[64] Vukadinovic, S., & Cvejic, S., (1996). *Mathematical Programming*. Univerzitet u Pristini, Pristina, In Serbian.

[65] Wang, C. M., (2004). *Comments on Two Direct Methods in Linear Programming*. Master Thesis, Windsor, Ontario, Canada.

[66] Wei, L., (2004). A note on two direct methods in linear programming. *Europ. J. Oper. Res., 158*, 262–265.

[67] Wolfram, S., (1991). *Mathematica: A System for Doing Mathematics by Computer.* Addison-Wesley Publishing Co, Redwood City, California.

[68] Wolfram, S., (1996). *Mathematica Book, Version 3.0.* Wolfram Media and Cambridge University Press.

[69] Wolfram, S., (1999). *The Mathematica Book* (4th edn.), Wolfram Media/Cambridge University Press.

[70] Wolfram, S. (2003). *The MATHEMATICA Book, 5th ed.*, Wolfram Media/Cambridge University Press, Champaign, IL 61820, USA.

[71] Wright, S. J., (1997). Primal-dual interior-point methods. Society for Industrial and Applied Mathematics. *Primal-Dual Interior-Point Methods.* SIAM, Philadelphia.

[72] Zang, Y., (1995). *User's guide to LIPSOL.* Department of Mathematics and Statistics, University of Maryland, Baltimore County, Baltimore, MD, USA.

Index

α_B, 65
α_N, 65
$\mathcal{A}_B$, 65
algoritam
    D2, 179
    Replace, 83
    SimplexStandardMin, 87
algorithm, 2
    An, 176
    dual simplex, 134
    ElJed, 141
    ElSl, 142
    RevBasicMax, 147
    RevNoBasicMax, 148
    SimplexStandardMax, 82

baza
    dopustiva, 65

Columns
    Duplicate, 172
columns

one-element, 172
cycling, 150

decision maker, 7
dependent restrictions, 171

function
    target, 22
    unlimited from below, 68

GEOM, 61

HOPDM, 32
hyperlink, 36

ideal values of objective
    functions, 6
inverse
    general, generalized, 178
    Moore-Penrose, 178

LOQO, 32
LINDO, 33
LIPSOL, 32

Printed in the United States
by Baker & Taylor Publisher Services

Printed in the United States
by Baker & Taylor Publisher Services